IMAGES OF ENGLAND

AROUND
HANLEY

IMAGES OF ENGLAND

AROUND HANLEY

JOHN S. BOOTH

TEMPUS

Frontispiece: A pottery paintress seen here in around 1910 producing fine decorative pottery to adorn houses large and small. Decorated wares produced in the Potteries were sent all over the world, gracing the tables of Kings and Emperors.

First published 2005

Tempus Publishing Limited
The Mill, Brimscombe Port,
Stroud, Gloucestershire, GL5 2QG
www.tempus-publishing.com

© John S. Booth, 2005

The right of John S. Booth to be identified as the Author
of this work has been asserted in accordance with the
Copyrights, Designs and Patents Act 1988.

All rights reserved. No part of this book may be reprinted
or reproduced or utilised in any form or by any electronic,
mechanical or other means, now known or hereafter invented,
including photocopying and recording, or in any information
storage or retrieval system, without the permission in writing
from the Publishers.

British Library Cataloguing in Publication Data.
A catalogue record for this book is available from the British Library.

ISBN 0 7524 3407 1

Typesetting and origination by Tempus Publishing Limited.
Printed in Great Britain.

Contents

	Acknowledgements	6
	Introduction	7
one	Streets, Squares and Buildings	11
two	Hanliensians: People of Hanley	47
three	Industry and Commerce	67
four	Churches and Religion	89
five	Parks	101
six	Entertainment	109
seven	Hanley District	119

Acknowledgements

The majority of pictures in this book are from my own collection of Hanley postcards, and much of the information is from my collection of North Staffordshire books and Hanley ephemera. I would like to thank John Bebbington for the loan of the Clarion Cycling Club and Hanley Wakes postcards.

Thanks also go to Josiah Wedgwood & Sons for their kind help with the Wedgwood pages, and to The Victorian County History for permission to reproduce two Hanley maps. I would also like to commend Steve Birks on the mine of information contained on his website www.thepotteries.org and thank him for checking the captions in this book. Many thanks also to Victoria Fenton for proofreading my work.

I would like to thank the staff at the Hanley Library Records Office for helping me find information on Bob Leivers, among other pleas for information. Also thanks to Jeff Kemp for pointing me in the right direction to research Hanley Swifts and the football pictures; to David Salt for information about his family; and to Mr M.J.H. Mills.

Lastly, many thanks to my wife and family for putting up with me talking about my book all the time.

Above: A distant view of Hanley from Hartshill church taken in about 1920. Bottle ovens and coal spoil heaps were a feature of the Hanley and District skyline during the late nineteenth and up to the mid-twentieth century.

Introduction

The earliest known written record of Hanley is in the 'Testa de Neville', written during the reign of Henry III (1216-1272), where it is written that William de Hanley had a fee farm paying six shillings a year and performing guard to the castle at Newcastle. Later in the far off history of Hanley, Henry, Earl of Richmond, while marching through North Staffordshire to do battle with Richard III at Bosworth Field (22 August 1485), ran short of provisions. He approached the miller of Shelton, who generously supplied him with the whole of his stock. Henry never forgot this favour and when he beat Richard III and became King Henry VII, he made a gift of his mill and millpond to the miller and ordered that he paid nothing in taxes to the nearby Newcastle in way of tenancy. Hanley and Shelton remained in the hands of local families (the Unwyn's, the Chatfield's, the Colclough's and the Bagnall's) through to the eighteenth century.

In the late seventeenth century, Hanley consisted of two small hamlets known as Hanley Upper Green, situated at the junction of Keelings Lane and Town Road, and Hanley Lower Green, where Market Square is today. By the 1750s, Hanley was making great advances from hamlet, to village, to small town, and many of the local potters became men of great wealth. Hanley was growing in importance too, but it didn't have a local government, or institution, or feast day, nothing to distinguish it from the other towns in the Potteries. Not having a Royal Charter, the local businessmen and potters of Hanley decided to make their own Charter of Corporation. Ephraim Chatterley, John Yates, John Badderley and other 'good men and true' resolved that Hanley would have its own mayor with civic honours.

In September 1783, a mayoral feast was held at the Swan Inn, Hanley, and Ephraim Chatterley was elected the first 'Mayor of Hanley'. The Duke of Sutherland, who lived at Trentham Hall, gave venison from his estate for the feast and this 'Venison Feast' is still held each year.

Hanley and Shelton appeared bracketed together from early times but it was not until 1813 that an Act of Parliament formed them into a market town. In 1825, another Act of Parliament formed Hanley's own police force, and in 1828 the Act was amended so that a head constable, three acting constables and six watchmen were appointed, with offices at the top of Trinity Street. By 1830 Hanley was considered a large market town, equal in size to the county town of Stafford. Industry and houses for the workers in the south-east area of Hanley, down Charles Street and Well Street, formed the district known as Wellington. Joiners Square existed as a few houses and collieries at the bottom of Lichfield Street on the southern edge of Hanley. Extensive developments along Keelings Lane and Upper Green towards the Caldon Canal became known as Northwood by 1832, and soon after came the districts known as Birches Head and Sneyd Green. In 1767, Josiah Wedgwood built a new pottery on Ridge House Estate, land he had acquired earlier. The first part of his pottery built on the site was known as Black Works, but he soon built a splendid new house and factory, which he named Etruria in honour of the ancient state in Italy. By 1841, Etruria was another thriving district of Hanley with Lord Granville's ironworks built close to Wedgwood's pottery works.

During the reign of Queen Victoria in 1857, Hanley and Shelton became the County Borough of Hanley with John Ridgway becoming its first mayor. The coat of arms for the new Borough of Hanley consisted of a shield split into three parts. The top left represented the pottery made in the area, while the top right represented the many chimneys of the coal, iron and pottery industries that were abundant in the new borough. The stars in the bottom third were taken from the original Wedgwood family coat of arms, and recognise the importance of Mr Wedgwood's pottery works in Etruria. The dromedary kneeling above the shield is from the Ridgway family coat of arms, recognising the great work that the Ridgway family had done in the area. The dromedary is retained in the coat of arms of the city of Stoke-on-Trent, occupying the top right corner.

When Katherine of Braganza married Charles II and brought a cask of tea leaves as part of her dowry, she could never have imagined the difference it would make to a small part of North Staffordshire. Pottery items began to grow in popularity and as drinking tea became more popular throughout the country, so the pottery industry grew with the demand for beautifully decorated tea ware. This led to a demand for decorative and ornamental pottery. Though it cannot compete with the more famous potteries of Burslem, Longton and Stoke, Hanley was the home of many excellent potters and pottery works. Josiah Wedgwood built his famous pottery at Etruria, G.L. Ashworth was an earthenware manufacturer in 1861 (he later made Mason's Patent Ironstone Pottery at the factory in Broad Street/Clough Street), and Dimmock's pottery occupied a site between Cheapside and Stafford Street in the heart of Hanley in 1830. Job Ridgway started his pottery at Cauldon Place, Shelton in about 1805, and his Cauldon pottery later became Brown-Westhead, Moore & Co. Clementson Brothers had the Bell works at the top of Broad Street on a site now occupied by the Stoke-on-Trent Museum. Samuel Hollins and partners founded the New Hall pottery in Shelton. John Glass was a well-known potter during the reign of Charles II and had his factory between what are now Glass Street and Town Road until 1835.

This factory was sold to Samuel Keeling and then to J. & G. Meakin, later moving to Ivy House Road and Lichfield Street. The Grimwade Brothers had their Winton pottery (later Royal Winton) in Shelton in 1889 and Messrs Fred and Alfred Johnson started Hanley pottery as Johnson Bros in about 1884. These are just a few of the well-known potters who carried out their business in the Hanley area.

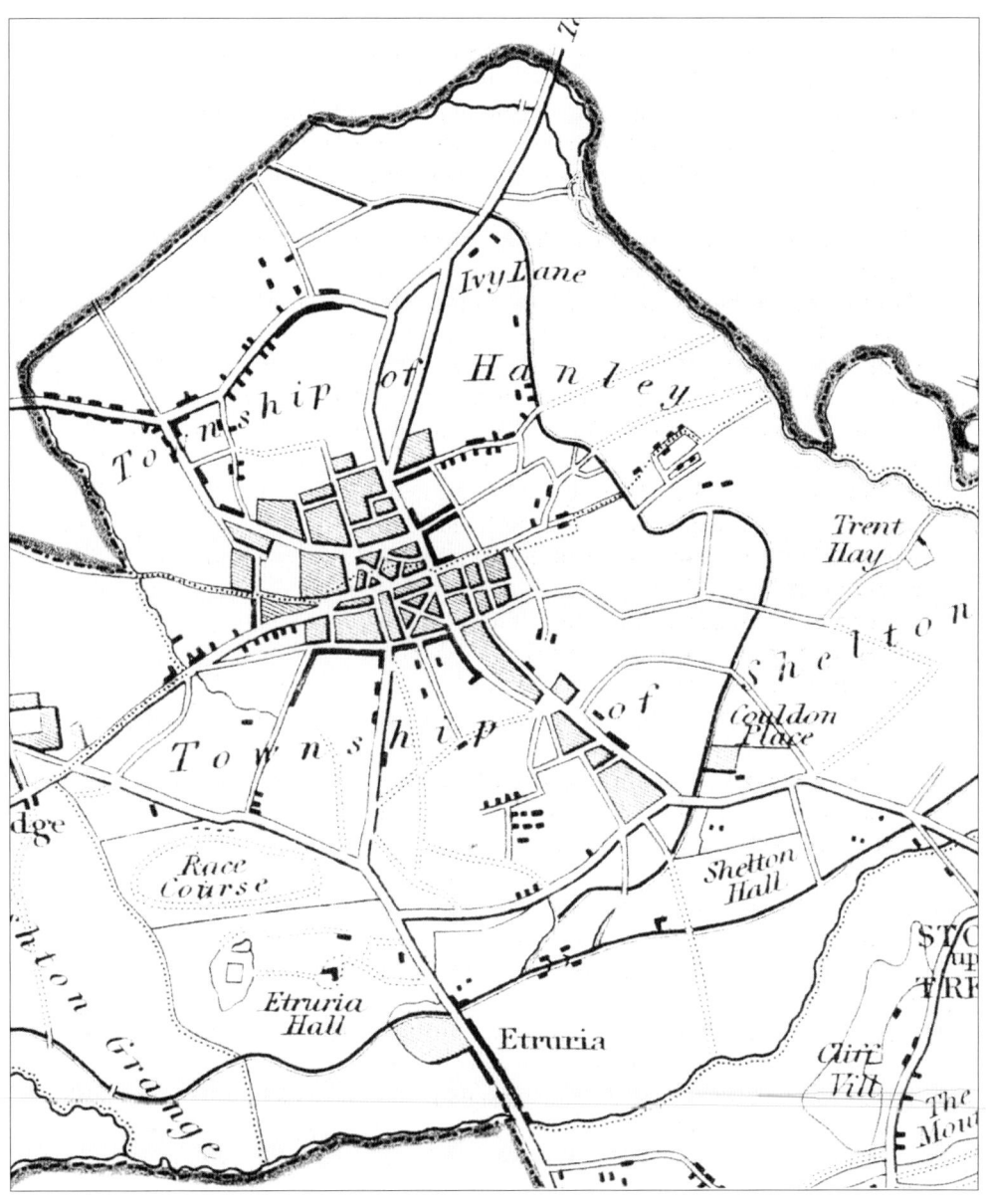

Taken from an engraving by J. & C. Walker (c. 1835)

There were also many industries that supported the pottery manufacturers. Thomas William Harrison worked in the flint mill owned by John Gerrard and later owned the business. The mill was situated in Bath Street (later Garth Street) alongside the Old Hall pottery. Mr Harrison, who then formed Harrison & Son (Hanley) Ltd, acquired both sites and built the company up to be one of the world's leading glaze and colour manufacturers, winning worldwide recognition. Another famous Hanley colour manufacturer was Wengers Ltd of Etruria. Founded by Mr A.F. Wenger in 1869, the firm was the first to manufacture liquid gold in England. Jesse Shirley established a flint and bone mill at Etruria in about 1820 where he calcined bone for use in the pottery industry, and in 1912 the company advertised specially prepared bone fertilisers for vine, lawn and horticultural purposes. Away from pottery, Henry Pidduck, a master clockmaker from Whitchurch, established a watchmaker and jeweller's shop in Market Square in 1841.

Many famous people were born in Hanley. Arnold Bennett, the author, was born on 27 May 1867 in Hope Street. He wrote many novels and plays, famously calling the six towns that make up Stoke-on-Trent 'the five towns'. Many of his novels, in which he called Hanley 'Hanbridge', were about the Potteries. Charles Butters, the auctioneer, was born in Hanley in 1832 and started his business in 1856. Gertie Gitana, the Music Hall star was born in Shirley Street, Longport, but her family moved to Fredrick Street in Hanley when she was three years old. In 1957, Fredrick Street was renamed Gitana Street in her honour. Commodore Edward John Smith was born in Well Street on 27 January 1850. As Commodore of the White Star Line he took command of the SS *Titanic* on its maiden voyage. The *Titanic* struck an iceberg late on 14 April 1912, and sank at 2.20 a.m. on 15 April with the loss of over 1,500 lives. Commander Smith went down with his ship. Footballer Sir Stanley Matthews was born on 1 February 1915 at 51 Seymour Street. Stan played for England fifty-four times and became the most famous footballer of his generation. The artist Peter De Wint was born in Hanley in 1784 to parents of Dutch origin, and today many public and private art collections proudly own a De Wint landscape.

The majority of pictures in this book were taken between 1900 and 1930, with a few exceptions either side of those dates. By this period, Hanley had grown into the largest of the Potteries towns, and the most central. In 1910, when the Potteries towns were federated into the City of Stoke-on-Trent, Hanley still thought itself the biggest and most important, though all Potteries-born people think that their town is better and more important to the history of the area. The back of one postcard sent to London reads 'Hanley has some beautiful buildings, just like London but much smaller of course.'

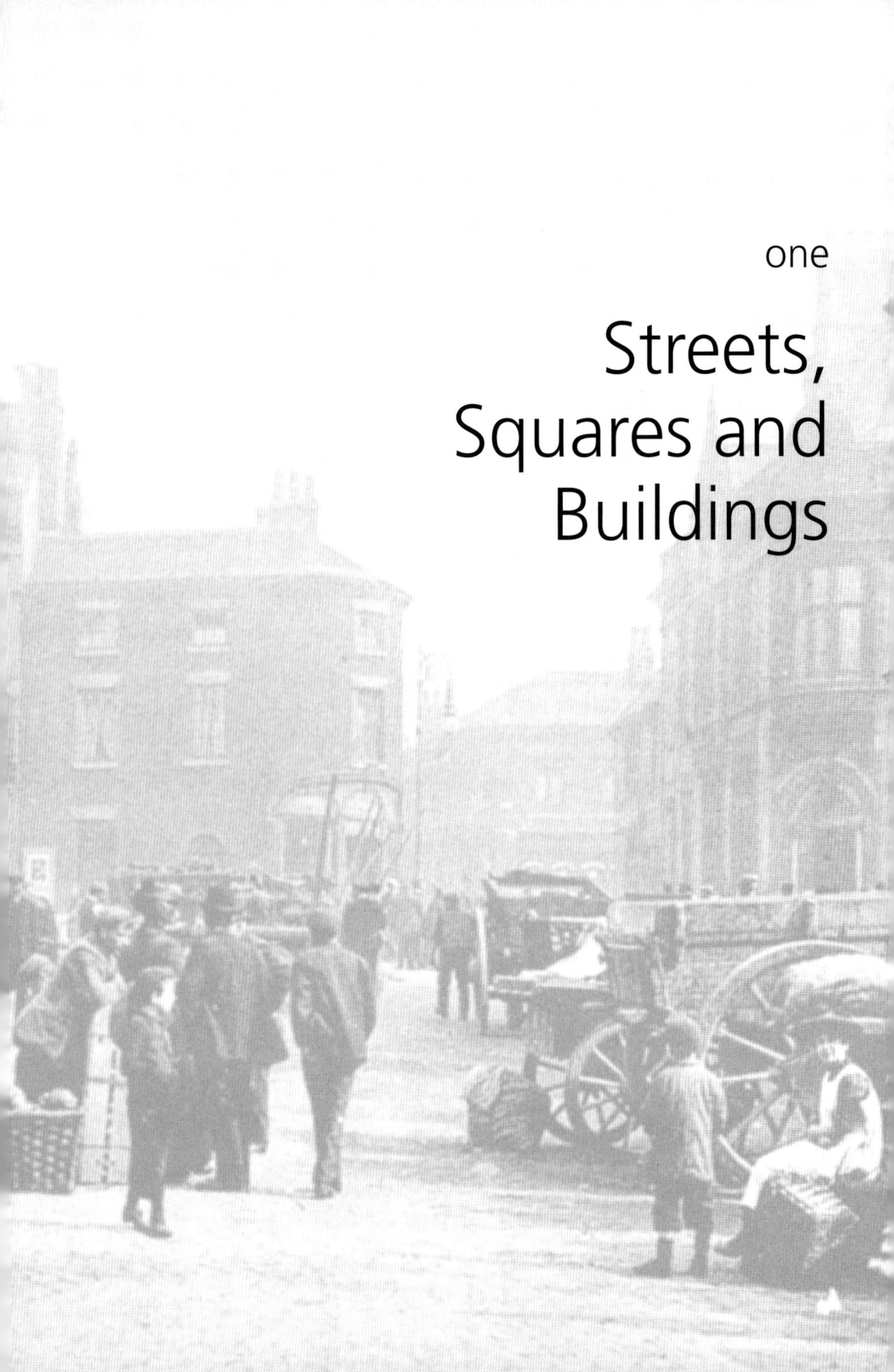

one

Streets, Squares and Buildings

By 1910, the Borough of Hanley covered an area of some 1,957 acres and consisted of the townships of Shelton, Birches Head, part of Sneyd Green, Northwood, Wellington, Joiners Square, Cliff Vale and a small part of Cobridge.

Hanley often maintains its links with the past through place names; for example, Birches Head is supposed to be named after a small grove of birch trees at the top of the hill where St Matthew's church now stands. Northwood and Eastwood were so-called after woodland known to have covered that area. There was also Bryan's Wood in the vicinity of Bryan Street and Winton Wood in the vicinity of Winton Street. According to Mr Blagg's history of the North Staffordshire Hunt, in about 1820 the hunt used to meet in Hanley's Market Square.

Hanley itself has seen little change to the layout of its streets since the early part of the nineteenth century. There seems to have been no planned layout for shops and commercial areas. During the nineteenth century there were still many dwellings in the centre of Hanley, including a few very fine houses owned by local pottery manufacturers, and even a windmill. When the windmill fell out of use its owner, Mr Dodd, turned it into an observatory and the Observatory Inn, on the brow of Hill Street (now Bucknall Old Road), occupies the site today.

Many of the streets and squares in Hanley have been named after people who have done good work in the town, or after pottery manufacturers. Garner Street is named after Robert Garner, who wrote the *Natural History of the County of Staffordshire* in 1844. Job Meigh was a founder of Bethesda, devoting time, energy and money to the church; Meigh Street is behind Woolworths by the Potteries Way.

A number of streets were named in honour of local potters; Glass Street after James Glass (*c.* 1762), Morley Street after Francis Morley (*c.* 1851), Mayer Street after Elijah Mayer (*c.* 1770) and Miles Bank after Thomas Miles, who was making brownware in about 1685. In 1780 George Broom left £1 a year to buy bread for the poor of Hanley, and his name survives today in Broom Street. Bagnall Street takes its name from a Mr Bagnall who owned a ship named *The Adventure*, which also accounts for the name of Adventure Place, a small street by the Victoria Hall. Well Street once had a well, and in the early nineteenth century an old man would draw water and sell it for one halfpenny per bucketful.

There are many books written containing a history of Hanley in which the reader can gain an insight into many of the other names associated with the town. The history of Hanley is truly fascinating.

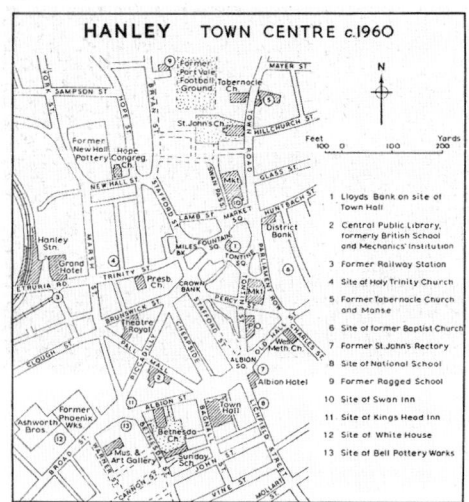

A map of Hanley town centre, *c.* 1960. Reproduced from the *Victoria County History, Staffordshire volume VIII*, Pp. 148, by permission of the Executive Editor.

A typical market day in Market Square, Hanley looking towards Lamb Street, *c.* 1925. Traders used their flat-bed lorries as ideal temporary market stalls. The large building to the right is the Indoor Market Hall. Note the policeman in the centre of the picture overlooking the market.

A view of Market Square, looking towards the indoor market and the Angel Vaults public house. Since 1776, Hanley has had full market rights and this fine indoor market hall, in a classic style with Doric columns, was built around 1831 for a cost of £3,500.

The Market Square on a quiet day. The shop in the centre is Pidduck & Sons, jewellers, which first opened in 1841 and was refurbished in the 1920s. Looking down to the left through Fountain Square is Crown Bank, and on to Piccadilly.

Another busy market day in the early 1920s, with produce stacked on the cobbled ground in large baskets and crates. If the market square was too full the traders pitched their wares in Upper Market Square and along Parliament Row.

Market Square in 1912, looking towards Upper Market Square. The large building in the background is The Angel Vaults, and beside it is The Grapes, where businessmen would meet over a drink on market days. Part of The Angel Vaults is still standing today and is used by The Abbey National Building Society.

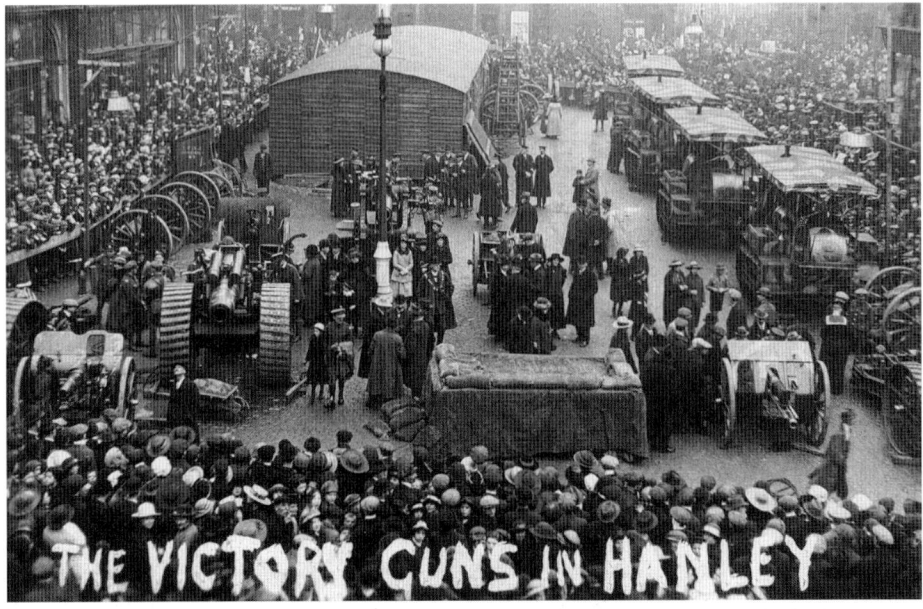

The same view of Market Square as in the picture above, but taken from an upstairs window in Pidduck's jewellers shop. This wonderful display of heavy armoury was held after the First World War and was a major attraction of the victory celebrations held throughout the country.

This view of Upper Market Square and the beginning of Parliament Row shows a typical market day. Children played an important role fetching and carrying on market days and tended to congregate around this prominent lamp waiting for work. This view looks up High Street towards the Tabernacle church and onward to Sneyd Green.

Sherwin's music shop sold records, musical instruments, sheet music and radios for household entertainment before television. Also, note the billboard carrier below advertising a new suit for twenty shillings.

Upper Market Square, showing goods being sold from the back of the horse-drawn carts that traders came to market on. Amies shop sold 'Society Boots', and next door is Williams & Bedworth, auctioneers.

More shops along Parliament Row; Amies is still selling 'Society Boots', but the auctioneer's has changed and is now home to The Lyric Electric Theatre. The Lyric opened in 1912 and showed silent films, but was closed by 1930. Next to The Lyric is an early Woolworths shop, which still occupies roughly the same site today.

A view of Upper Market Square and part of Parliament Row taken from Tontine Square. The building in the centre of the picture is The District Bank. The low wall in front of the bank was a meeting place and somewhere to sit and watch the world go by on market days.

Left: Sherratt's Cash Grocers shop occupies a prominent spot in Upper Market Square, *c.* 1920. As can be seen on the outside of the shop, Mr Sherratt was a grocer and a tea blender, amongst other things. Recent years have seen the shop become a television rental outlet and a sandwich shop.

Below: Upper Market Square, with Sherwin's music shop on the left and The Angel Vaults and The Grapes public houses on the right. Running up the middle of the cobbles on High Street (now Town Road) are tramlines. The tall building at the top of High Street is the Tabernacle church.

Further up High Street, with a closer look at the Tabernacle church in the centre of the picture. Below the Tabernacle to the left is the Hanley church of St John's, and below the church is the side of the indoor market.

Lower down Fountain Square in about 1920, showing the bronze statue of a Greek maiden presented to Hanley in 1859 by Mayor William Brownfield. In 1920 the statue was moved to Northwood Park, but it was returned to the square in the mid-1970s.

A view of Market Square from Fountain Square, showing the full frontage of the indoor market in the centre of the picture. This lovely Gothic-style market building was built in 1849. Pidduck & Son's jewellers shop is on the left. Henry Pidduck was the mayor of Hanley in 1864.

Victoria House is on the right; once the home of T. & R. Gilman, tailors, hatters and hosiers, it is now occupied by The Woolwich Building Society on the ground floor and the Potteries Resource Centre above.

Fountain Square just after 1920, without the bronze statue. During market days traders used the square to sell trees and plants. Victoria House, on the right, has changed hands since the earlier picture; Gilman's have gone and The Halifax Building Society has moved in.

This view of Fountain Square in about 1915 was taken from the front of the Old Town Hall, and shows that most of the shops seem to sell clothing. On the left we see Batchelor's tailors and costume shop and Stead & Simpson's shoe shop. Across the tramway, Cash & Co. sell boots and shoes, SMC sell shirts and overalls and Marsden Bros also sell boys clothes. Fountain Square was also the early home of *The Staffordshire Advertiser*.

Fountain Square, looking down towards Crown Bank and Piccadilly. The buildings on the left still stand today. The public house still carries the name of Ye Olde French Horn, although the shop below is now a fast-food outlet.

Until the latter part of the nineteenth century, Hanley Old Town Hall occupied the eastern corner of Fountain Square. The town hall, built in a classical style, was attacked during the Chartist Riots of 1842 as the Riot Act was read from the steps to the protesters gathering outside. The building was sold to Lloyds Bank in 1886 and demolished during the mid-1930s, when the present Lloyds Bank was built in its place.

Looking from Miles Bank towards the Old Town Hall. McIlroy's General Store, a forerunner of the modern department store, is on the left. Stead & Simpson's shoe shop and Johnson Brothers', cleaners, are on the right.

Hanley Old Town Hall was opened in the early 1840s and was built on the site of the old Butter Market. The building was also used as a police station, with cells for the temporary confinement of prisoners in the basement. The ground floor contained a spacious entrance hall with a newsroom on one side and a council chamber on the other. The building cost £5,500 to build.

Part of the front of McIlroy's store from the bottom of Miles Bank. Known as 'The People's Providers', McIlroy's started business in 1883 and sold the shop to Lewis's in 1935. The tram in the centre is advertising Lipton's Tea, and Greenwood's outfitters shop is on the right.

Lower down Miles Bank, showing a better view of Greenwood's outfitters. The shop still operates from a similar corner today, though it is now in a modern precinct.

At the side of these old houses is the end of a passage that leads from Stafford Street to the new post office in Tontine Street and Tontine Square. This row of houses was demolished in the early 1920s to make way for new shops.

A view of Stafford Street, *c.* 1910, showing the corner of Lamb Street in the centre of the picture. The pottery factory in the distance was occupied by Bishop & Stonier, earthenware manufacturers.

By the late 1930s Lewis's department store had built a modern new building on the site of the pottery works and moved from the old McIlroy's shop. A new building then replaced McIlroy's, although neither building stands today.

Looking up Lamb Street from Stafford Street towards Market Square. Lamb Street was originally named to commemorate the work done for Hanley by the Revd Lamb.

Looking halfway down Lamb Street from the bottom of Market Square. M. Huntbach & Co. had a store on the left going down Lamb Street and later moved across the road to occupy one of the largest department stores in Hanley. W.S. Brown & Sons, butchers, are in a shop in Stafford Street, across from the bottom of Lamb Street. Brown also had a butcher's shop in Broad Street.

Still standing in Tontine Square today is this typical 1930s-style building. When this picture was taken W.H. Ball & Sons were having a week of 'Special Offers On Dining Room Furniture'. Today it is the home of The Halifax Building Society.

Built of stone from the Waterloo stone quarry at Alton, Hanley's new post office was opened on 18 October 1906. The post office must be one of the few buildings in Hanley that will soon be able to boast one hundred years of public use without a change of function.

Left: In 1912, the shop to the left of the post office was Hill & Ainsworth's, printers and stationers. Later the premises were taken over by Webberley's, printers and bookshop. The shop on the right of the post office was Henry Turner's butchers shop.

Below: The current Hanley Town Hall can be found in Albion Street. Built of red brick and stone in 1864 and designed by Robert Scrivener, it started life as The Queens Hotel and became Hanley Town Hall during the 1880s. The Borough of Hanley coat of arms can be seen above the entrance.

Going back down Stafford Street is Crown Bank, where the large building on the left of the picture still stands today. Occupied for a long time by Dunn's, the gentleman's outfitters, it is today a hairdressers. On the left of the picture is a stop from which buses continue to pick up passengers.

Left: Opposite the entrance to the town hall is the Hanley War Memorial. Harold Brownsword was a renowned London sculptor who was born in Hanley. He was commissioned to design the war memorial in 1921. The bronze figure of Victory holds a sword encircled by a wreath in her right hand, with a plumed helmet on her head and a shield behind her left leg. The snake beneath her feet alludes to the defeat of evil, while the lion on her helmet and the two Tudor roses around the Stoke-on-Trent coat of arms symbolise the English nation.

Below: In 1914 there was also a bus stop on the other side of Stafford Street. According to the writing on the back of this postcard, the large crowd of men in the middle of the picture has gathered for a First World War recruitment campaign.

Crown Bank from the top of Piccadilly. On the left is the Dolphin Hotel and in the middle is North Staffordshire Furniture Mart, house furnisher, run by J. Miller, established in 1840. To the right is the Marquis of Granby public house.

A later picture of the Dolphin Hotel, here in the middle of the picture. Notice that Miller's furniture shop has changed hands and is now Capper's Ltd, grocers.

Crown Bank, looking towards the original premises of Boot's Cash Chemist, with Brunswick Street down to the right and Piccadilly to the left. Burton's, gentlemens outfitters, operated from these corner-premises until the 1980s. Boot's Chemist moved to Parliament Row around 1930.

Half-way down Crown Bank, looking towards Piccadilly and Broad Street during the early 1920s. The prominent building with a clock beneath its small spire is still a Hanley landmark today. Many of these lovely old buildings are still standing.

Outside Burton's gentlemens outfitters was the place where the majority of buses left Hanley for Shelton and Stoke. During recent roadworks some of the cobbles seen in this picture were revealed under the modern tarmac.

Many of these shops at the top of Piccadilly are still standing today, although Boot's Chemist later moved to Parliament Row. The public house next to Adams & Co. is one of the oldest still open in Hanley.

Half-way down Piccadilly, looking towards Crown Bank. Note the shop window on the left belonging to The Universal Coloured Trading Stamp Co. The window states that no goods are sold and that everything is given away in exchange for stamps.

This tram has reached the bottom of Piccadilly, where Broad Street begins its journey towards Stoke. The Kings Head public house (here seen on the right) was later demolished, although many of these shops remain today.

Pall Mall, Hanley

Pall Mall crosses Piccadilly about half-way down. On one side were modest shops and houses, (above) while on the other side stood the far grander Hanley School of Art, the Public Free Library and North Staffordshire Technical and Art Museum (below). The public library was established in 1887 and the museum was opened during 1891, but by the 1970s both buildings were emptied and their contents moved to new buildings in Bethesda Street.

PALL MALL, FREE LIBRARY & SCHOOL OF ART, HANLEY.

The junction of Pall Mall and Piccadilly, showing Arnot's tobacconist shop on the right. The shop just above Arnot's is Frank Fernie's hatters (notice the large bowler hat above the door). The shop on the left, J.C. Schofield's, is an ironmonger's.

The Rose and Thistle beer house, in the centre of this picture, is situated on the corner of Pall Mall opposite Arnot's tobacconist shop. The tram on the left, advertising Bovril, is on its way to Shelton and Stoke.

A better view of The Rose and Thistle. The ironmonger's shop below advertises the goods on sale outside the shop.

The opposite side of Piccadilly, showing the Cash Clothing Company shop on the corner of Pall Mall. Below the clothing shop are the premises of Mrs J. Baker, fruiterer and game dealer, with a sign above the shop advertising fruit from Covent Garden.

HIGHER GRADE SCHOOL, HANLEY.

This school in Hanley (above and below) was originally established as a higher grade school for boys and girls and opened on 6 April 1894. Situated between Old Hall Street and Birch Terrace, it came under the Education Act of 1902 and was officially recognised as a secondary school, but in 1924 a further change of title gave the school its most remembered name, Hanley High School. The school became a boys-only school in 1938 when the girls were transferred to the new Thistley Hough School for Girls. The building was vacated in 1939 after being declared unsafe, with the boys first moving to Brownhills High School, then to Chell, and finally in 1953 to Bucknall.

From the top of Miles Bank, looking towards Stafford Street and showing the wonderful building occupied by Teeton's, silk and linen merchants. This building still stands today, with the Yorkshire Bank on the ground floor.

The long frontage of McIlroy's wrapped around the corner of Stafford Street and Fountain Square. In this pre-1920 picture, the bronze fountain and Old Town Hall can be seen in the background.

A First World War tank was displayed near the top of Charles Street for a number of years after the war.

Taken from the top of Lamb Street, this picture (c. 1920) shows that the middle of Market Square was used for car parking when it was not a market day. The entrance to M. Huntbach & Co.'s shop is under the glass canopy on the left.

two

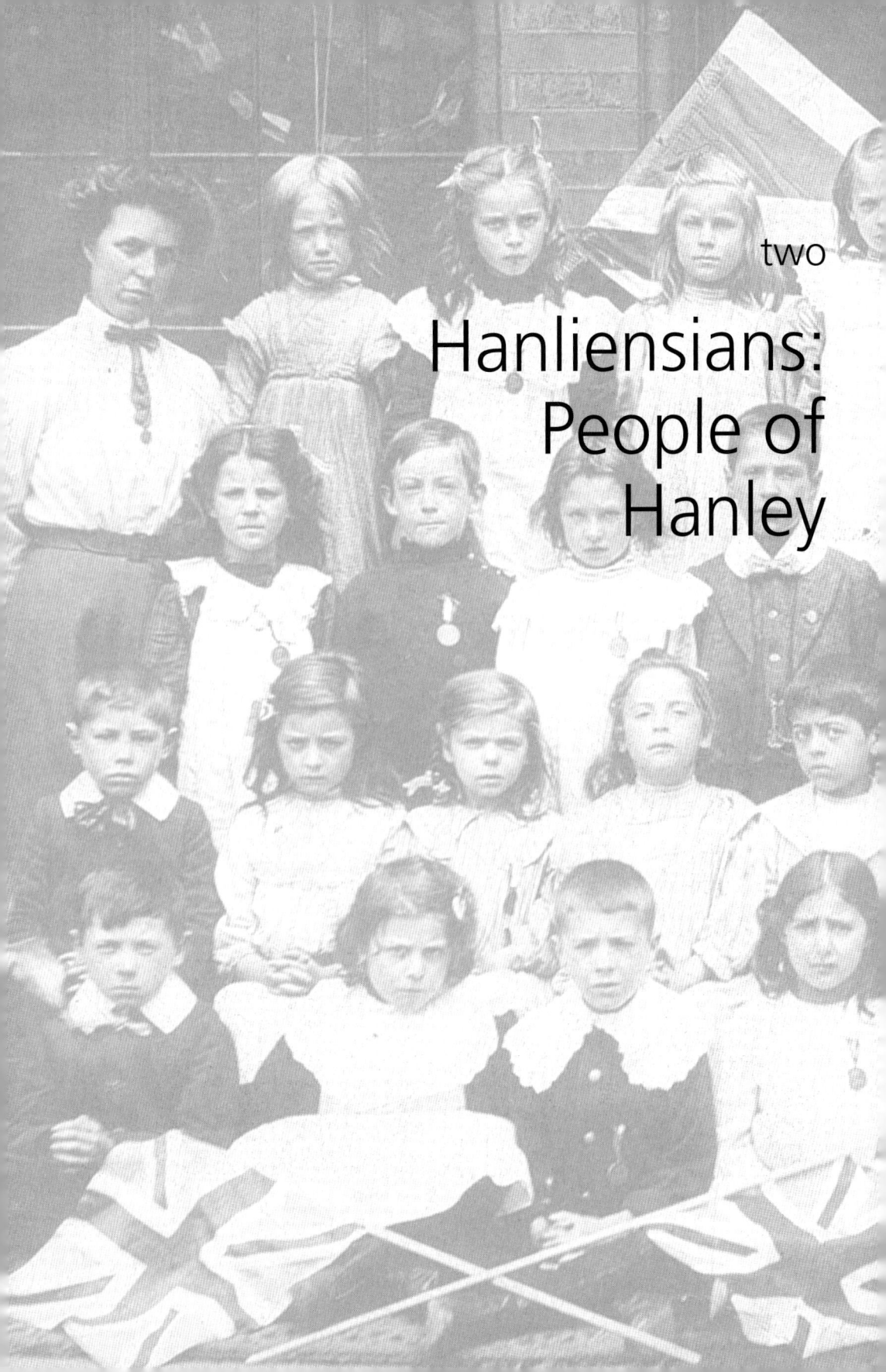

Hanliensians: People of Hanley

The people born and bred in Hanley are passionately proud of their home; to them it is the biggest and the best of the six Potteries towns. This, of course, is a matter of opinion as the town where you are born is your home and you are quite naturally proud of it.

Hanley can boast of being the birthplace of some very famous people - not only potters, but a world famous writer, an artist, a sea commodore and, of course, the most famous footballer of them all. Much has been written about these famous people so I'll just skate over a few facts. Arnold Bennett was born 27 May 1867 at 90 Hope Street, Hanley, which was at that time a pawnshop. He spent much of his early life with his grandparents in St John's Square, Burslem and made the Potteries known throughout the world through his excellent novels about the area. He died in 1931.

Peter De Wint was born in 1784 of a Dutch father who had a doctor's practice in Hanley. He was originally destined to become a doctor like his father but showed an early interest in art, eventually persuading his father to let him study art in London. In 1802 he was indentured to John Raphael Smith to be taught the art of engraving and portrait painting. His topographical watercolours grace many private collections and his work is much sought after by art collectors.

Born on 27 January 1850 in Well Street, Edward John Smith, became Commodore of the White Star Line by 1912, despite being born so far from the sea. Educated at Etruria British School, he left school at the age of twelve and started work at the Etruria forge. In 1871, he left Hanley and was apprentice in Liverpool to A. Gibson and Co., and by 1874 he had gained his Masters Certificate in Seamanship. He joined the White Star Line in 1880 and rose to Commodore of the White Star Fleet by 1912. In April 1912 he was captain of the ill-fated *Titanic* on its maiden voyage to America.

Stanley Matthews was born 1 February 1915, son of Jack Matthews, the 'fighting barber from Hanley'. Jack had a barber's shop at 7 Market Street and was a well-known featherweight boxer with 350 fights to his credit. Stan went to Wellington Road School and played football for the school team. At the age of fourteen he was chosen to play for England Schoolboys, and he signed for Stoke City at fifteen years of age. He made his debut for Stoke City at seventeen and made his full England debut at nineteen. He played professional football for thirty-three years and was never cautioned once. He was the first footballer to be knighted, and Sir Stanley died, aged eighty-five, in 2000.

Listed below are a few of the locally well known people and potters born in Hanley:

Charles Butters, Auctioneer (1832—1891)
James Dudson, Pottery Manufacturer (1818—1882)
Francis Emery, Colour Manufacturer (1792—1857)
John Ridgway, Pottery Manufacturer (1785—1860)
Jesse Shirley, Flint Grinder & Bone Merchant (1848—1927)
Thomas William Twyford, Pottery Manufacturer (1849—1921)

Stanley Matthews was born in Hanley on 1 February 1915, and in his own words he was 'mad about football'. While sitting at his desk at Wellington Road School he couldn't wait for the four o'clock bell to ring so he could play football in the strip of wasteland opposite his house. Stan's father was an athletics fan and entered Stan in the 100 yards race in the Stoke-on-Trent sports. Stan won through the heats, eventually winning the final, with prizes of a gold watch and two goldfish. At fourteen, both Port Vale and Stoke City were watching Stan's football progress. Stan used to watch Port Vale at the Hanley Recreation Ground, his hero at the time being Bob Connelly, the Vale centre half. Because of his hero, Stan used to play centre half for his school team but he was switched to right-wing when he scored eight of the goals in a thirteen-goal win. On the advice of his father Stan signed for Stoke City, though he continued to watch Port Vale. Stan first played for the First XI, aged nineteen, against Bury, where Stoke won 1—0. The rest, as they say, is football history. In 1948, Stan wrote a book about his life called *Feet First*; every football fan should read it.

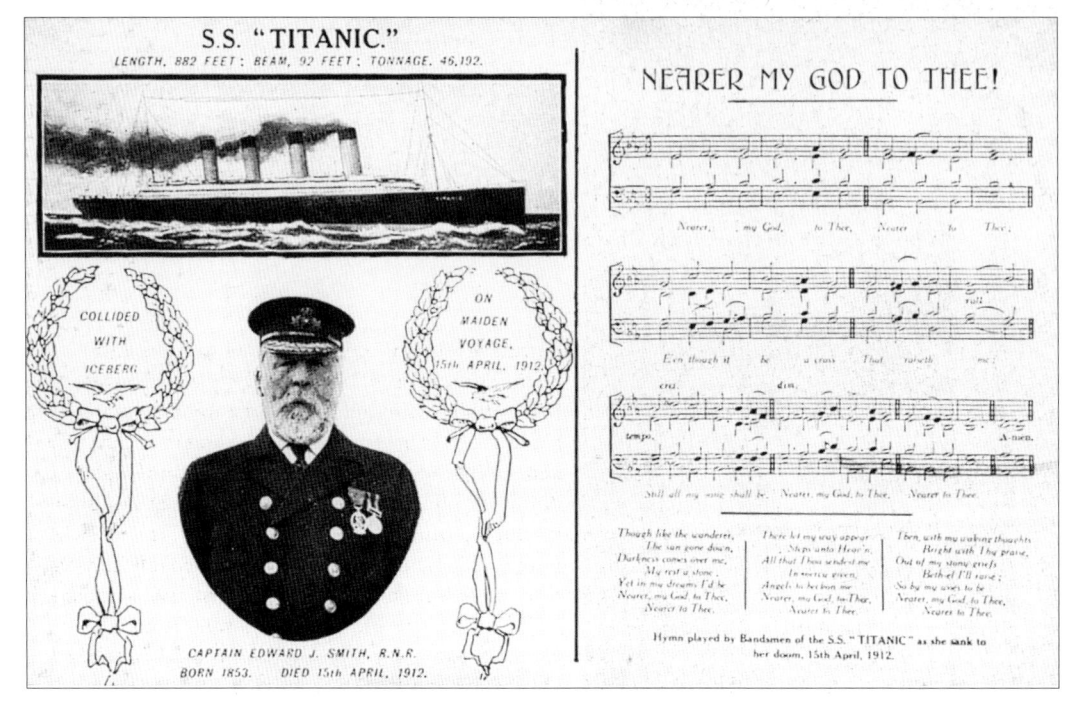

Edward John Smith was born in Well Street, Hanley on 27 January 1850. He left Etruria School at the age of twelve and spent the next nine years working at the Etruria forge. It is said that he was always interested in the sea, and he left Hanley for Liverpool to study seamanship. In 1874, at the age of twenty-four, he gained his Masters Certificate which allowed him to seek work on the sea. His first command was *The Lucy Fennel*, and in March 1880 he joined the White Star Line. He first served aboard freight-liners to Australia but it was obvious to those around him that he was a formidable ship's captain. He quickly grew in importance in the White Star Line and became captain of the *Adriatic*, *Celtic*, *Coptic* and the *Germanic* amongst others. He was captain of the *Majestic* for nine years and was awarded the Transport Medal. He was an honorary commander in the Royal Naval Reserve and regarded as a safe captain among his fellow shipmates. He was awarded the Royal Distinction in 1910 and in 1912 was awarded the prestigious command of the *Titanic*. There have been many films about that fateful maiden voyage, but true history will report that he was a brave man, last seen at the helm of the *Titanic* and going down with his ship, making no attempt to save himself. A statue of Captain Smith stands overlooking the bowling green in a park in Lichfield, and every April a wreath is laid at the base.

At fifteen years of age, Bob Leivers won his first Staffordshire swimming title and became the first Staffordshire swimmer to 'beat the minute' (swim 100 yards in less than a minute). For the next decade he and another local swimmer, Norman Wainwright, dominated British swimming. Bob held Staffordshire swimming titles in three different styles, and in 1932 (while still attending Longton High School) he went to the Los Angeles Olympics, the first ever schoolboy to be selected for the British Olympic Team. The name of Bob Leivers was, for the next four years, at the forefront of British swimming.

Following the Los Angeles Olympics, Bob swam in the European Championships and the Empire Games. His second Olympics were the 1936 Berlin Olympics, where Bob was a finalist in three events, and was the fastest European swimmer in the 1,500 metres. At the 1938 Empire Games (held in Sydney, Australia) he won the 1,650 yards freestyle in 19 minutes 46.6 seconds, breaking the existing Australian record for the event. Though born in Nottingham, his family moved to the Eastwood district of Hanley when he was very young. At one time, Bob held every English freestyle swimming title from 220 yards upwards. When his swimming career ended, Bob became the swimming instructor for the Stoke-on-Trent ATC. Bob died in 1964.

A wonderful picture of Cobridge Church of England Infants Class 2, taken in 1924, showing the children during the unrest of political upheaval and strikes. Local miners and potters were affected by industrial disputes and the children of the day put on a brave face.

This group of children from Hope Street Infants are all dressed up to celebrate the coronation of King George V in 1911. All the children proudly wear the medallions given to them by the local school board to commemorate the coronation.

Left: Spencer Cartlidge outside the front of 178 Cobridge Road, Hanley, in 1942. Being a veteran of the First World War, Spencer wanted to help his country during the Second World War. He told his family that he was a night-watchman for a local toy shop, but after the war he revealed that he was a security guard at a Rolls Royce depot. The picture shows him in his security guard uniform.

Below: Spencer and his wife Vronwyn (on the right) stand with their son John in his RAF Navigators flying suit. Between them is daughter Joan, who worked as a GPO Telephonist.

Stoke-on-Trent 'Gun Week' comes to Hanley, with artillery guns displayed at the top of Lamb Street in November 1918. Known nationally as 'Feed the Guns Week', this was a way to get people to buy War Bonds. The week started in Market Square on Monday 4 November 1918, the same day that Austria signed the Armistice and left Germany to fight alone. The war ended the following Monday on 11 November. In fact, the guns were still in Hanley when the Armistice was signed, providing a poignant backdrop for speeches and celebrations. 'Gun Week' was opened by the mayor and Sir Joseph

Cook. The total collected in the Potteries was £1,221,911, which exceeded the £1,123,000 raised during an earlier 'Tank Week". From left to right, back row: Miss Bond, Miss Smith, Miss Stevenson, Mr Gleaves, Mr Berlyn, Miss Littler, Mrs Allman, Miss Hughes. Front row: Miss Robinson, Mr Perry, Miss Martin. It is recorded that £56,445 11s 0d was raised during the week in Hanley.

A picture of Beaty Cartlidge on her wedding day, taken on the steps of 38 East View, Hanley, in December 1939. Beaty married Albert Booth before he went off to war.

During the war years, Beaty, like lots of other women at the time, 'did her bit' by working on the buses while her husband fought in France. Many women worked in jobs that meant men could be released to join the army.

The back garden of 113 Chell Street, a prefabricated house built just after the Second World War. The top picture shows Ann and Gill Goodall with their cousins Keith and John Booth proudly sitting on their tricycles. In the picture below, Gill holds the wheelbarrow while John fills it up. Both these pictures were taken around 1946, just after the Booth family moved into the house, which was halfway down a row of about eleven 'prefabs'. Very modern for the time, each had central heating, a gas fridge and gas oven in a fitted kitchen, with a small garden at the front and a large garden at the back. When the prefabs were taken down in the mid-sixties, an entrance to Hanley Forest Park was built in their place.

Since the Chartist years of the 1840s, Hanley seems to have been a focal point for protests. The above picture was taken during the early part of the Second World War, with people protesting against the conflict.

An election rally just after the war, passing down Fountain Square. These rallies usually started with an open-air meeting in Market Square.

In February 1894 six young men met in Birmingham and formed the Socialists' Cycling Club; after their second meeting they changed the name to the Clarion Cycling Club, after their favourite 'penny weekly' paper. By the end of 1894, there were four other Clarion Cycling Clubs, one each in the Potteries, Liverpool, Bradford and Barnsley. By 1895 there were thirty Clarion Cycling Clubs throughout Britain, and seventy by 1897, at a time when cycling was one of the most popular pastimes in the country. The Potteries Clarion Cycling Club held their meetings at Hanley Working Men's Club (above) and the club remained popular until the 1930s.

In its early days, the cycling club members were predominantly men, but after the turn of the century, women enjoyed the cycling pursuits too. The Potteries Clarion Cycling Club used to cycle out to different places of interest where they would meet other Clarion Cycling Clubs for a social gathering and lunch. Note all the cycles leaning against the building on the right (below).

Left: Born in Chelmsford, Essex in 1843, Thomas William Harrison worked for and later owned the pottery colours and glazes manufactory of John Gerrard in Bath Street. Thomas became a member of the Hanley School Board in 1888, believing passionately in education. Elected chairman in 1896, he was a strong supporter of building a new Higher Grade School in Hanley. He lived at The Hollies in Northwood and died in 1919.

Below: The funeral of Edward John Ridgway in 1896 as it passes through Upper Market Square. Edward John was the grandson of Job Ridgway and owned the Bell works in Hanley, which were later sold to Joseph Clementson.

Though not born in Hanley (she was born in Longport in 1887), Gertie Gitana considered Hanley to be her home after her family moved to Fredrick Street when she was young. Gertie was very proud when Fredrick Street was renamed Gitana Street in her honour. A famous music hall star, Gertie started her stage career at the tender age of four when she joined Tomkinson's Royal Gypsy Children's Troupe which was very popular in the Potteries. She was soon billed as 'England's Premier Midget Comedienne' but her mother protested at the wording and the billing was changed. She was later called 'The Wonderful Little Gitana' (Gitana is the Italian feminine for Gypsy).

Gertie was a natural on the stage, and was soon billed as a dance artiste, singer, Tyrolean yodeller, male impersonator and paper tearer; she was very popular with the audience and her talent was obvious. At eight, she left the troupe and the Potteries to tour the country with her own act under the wing of a Mrs O'Connor who, with her husband, managed Music Hall acts. Gertie sang such famous songs as *Nellie Dean* and *When I Leave the World Behind*, and became one of the most famous music hall stars of the day.

During the First World War, many photographs of proud soldiers were staged in a local photographers' studio and made into postcards so they could be sent home as a family keepsake. On the right is Sergeant James Roden of the Shropshire Light Infantry, who later lived in Broad Street.

During the 1930s James Roden and his family lived behind their Broad Street pet shop. He was well known in the local community as a brave old soldier who had achieved the rank of Regimental Colour Sergeant.

Above: William Simpson Cartlidge, a compositor with the *Staffordshire Sentinel*, proudly sits with his wife Emily Grace and their daughters Alice, Fanny, Gertrude and Agnes, c. 1890. These 'cabinet' photographs were very popular in the late 1800s and are valuable today, showing, not least, how our ancestors dressed at the time.

Left: This cabinet photograph is of Thomas Roberts, his wife Ann and their two small children. Thomas was a Welsh coal miner born in Holywell, North Wales, who moved to Hanley to find work in our local coal mines. In 1891 he lived at 95 Rose Street, Northwood with his family of four and worked at Hanley Deep Pit.

Opposite: This fine gentleman stands in his North Staffordshire Railway uniform alongside some railway trucks. The North Staffordshire Railway, or 'Knotty' as it was affectionately known, was formed around 1845 and had a station in Hanley.

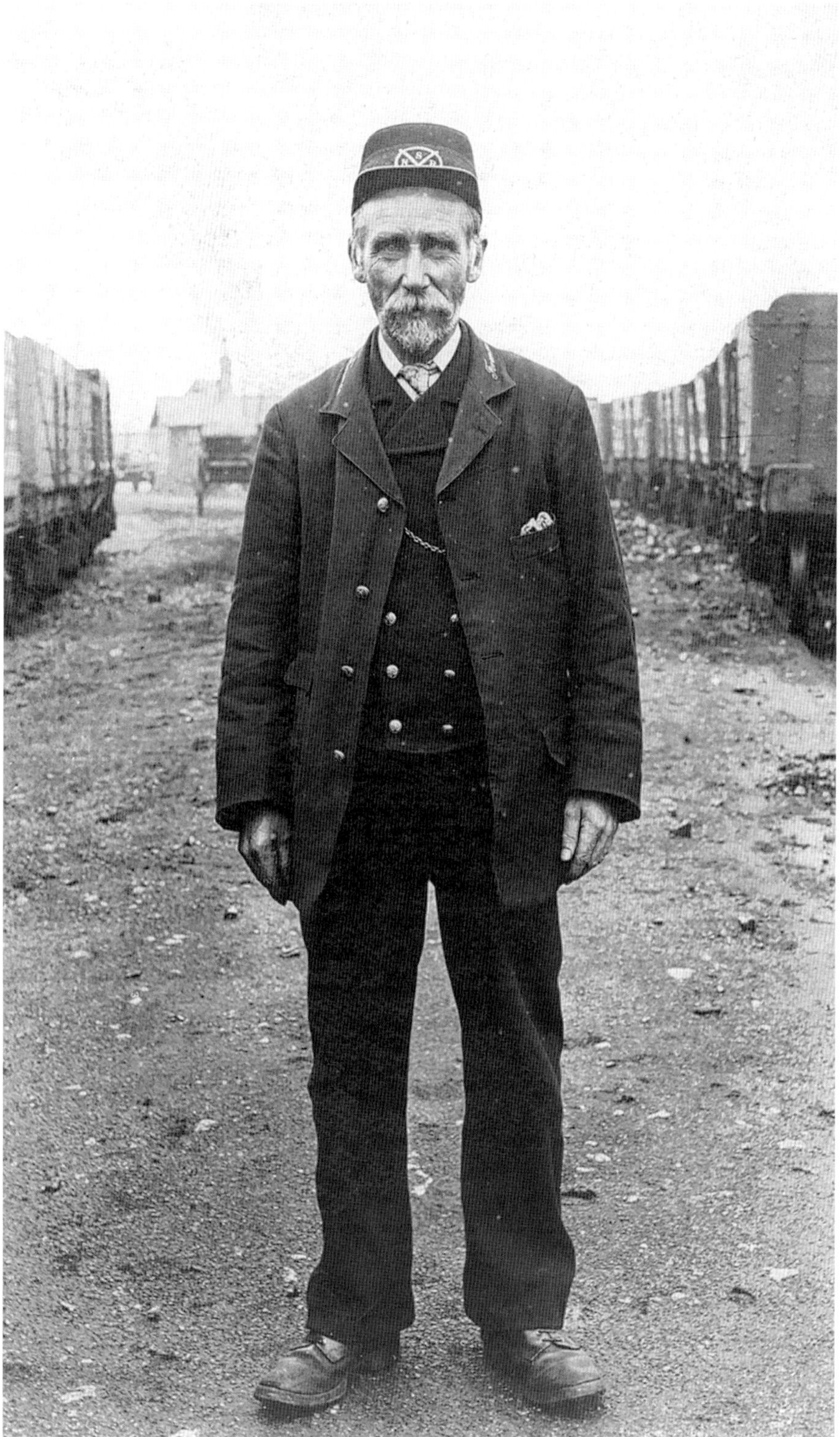

The modelling class at Hanley School of Art, seen in 1908. Students came from all over the country to be taught all aspects of ceramic art, drawing, painting and modelling. Many famous pottery artists and modellers attended Hanley School of Art before furthering their education in London or abroad. Charles Vyse won a scholarship to the Royal College of Art while attending Hanley, later opening a studio in London. His slip cast models of London life have become much sought after. Reginald Hagger attended Hanley School of Art, as did ceramic artists Dora Billinton and Norah Braden, both pioneers of British women's pottery. Many of the local pottery owners were patrons of the school and gave it their full support.

According to Kelly's *The Potteries*, Primrose Motor Coaches used to operate from a garage in Stoke Road, Shelton. Known as charabancs, these long-wheelbase open coaches were popular during the 1920s, taking people on trips to local beauty spots.

three

Industry and Commerce

Since the earliest days, Hanley seems to have been at the centre of trade and commerce in the Potteries. By 1783, the town was growing at such a great rate that the wealthy men of the town felt a little humbled that their town did not have its own local government. They therefore created a Charter of Corporation and municipal honours for Hanley. This Hanley Corporation held meetings to govern the town and elected its own mayor. This situation carried on until 1857 when Hanley became a county borough. In 1812, an Act of Parliament was obtained for enlarging and regulating the market. The Act authorised markets to be held on Wednesdays and Saturdays, with the latter being the principle market day. By 1841, Pigot's Directory of England called Hanley 'a large modern market town with its own meat market'.

Pottery factories close to the town centre included Dimmock's Albion Works, situated between Stafford Street and Cheapside, Ashworth's (also known as Mason's) between Broad Street and Clough Street, Ridgeway's and later Clementson's Bell works at the top of Broad Street. John Mare had a pottery in Miles Bank, while Job Meigh and later Charles Whitehead made pottery at the Old Hall works in Bath Street (now Garth Street), which later became Harrison's Phoenix chemical works. On the outskirts of the town were many other 'pot banks': Wedgwood's in Etruria, Brown Westhead, Moore & Co. at Cauldon pottery in Shelton, Johnson Bros, Imperial Pottery and J. & G. Meakin's pottery at Ivy House. These are just a few of the world-famous potters who worked in Hanley. Keates & Co. (who made gazetteers of counties throughout England) had a printers in Brunswick Street, Ratauds Ltd printed ceramic transfers in Parker Street and Jesse Shirley had (and still has) a flint mill in Etruria. William Walker started to manufacture all kinds of oils and greases in Century Street, G. Wooliscroft made tiles in Mellville Street and Etruria, and Goodwin's foundry was established in 1883. The list could go on and on. Of the well known local stores in Hanley that started trading in the nineteenth century, were Louis Taylor & Sons auctioneers (established 1877) and Gilman's tailors (established 1846). M. Huntbach & Co., Bratt & Dyke's, McIlroy's and Henry Pidduck & Son, jewellers, were all still going strong in 1908. Hanley, by this time, was (and still is) the largest town in the Potteries.

The smoke of Hanley in its industrial heyday. Shelton church can be seen on the left.

W. S. BROWN & SONS LTD.

BROAD STREET, HANLEY, STOKE-ON-TRENT

Brown's have had a butcher's shop in Broad Street for many years and only closed it in the later part of the twentieth century.

The back of this 1912 postcard states that this is a picture of the wedding of a member of W. S. Brown's family; the bride and groom are sitting on the grass in the middle of the front row.

Close to the corner of Crown Street is 29 Broad Street, the high-class tailor's shop of R. Hastings Ross and Co., seen here with the proud owner standing outside. The Ross family lived behind. Above the shop is now a fast food outlet.

At 93 Broad Street was the newsagents and tobacconist shop of Thomas Salt. Thomas occupied the shop from 1881 but it had been a stationer's shop since 1871. He lived there with his second wife and their three children. His wife probably kept the shop while he plied his trade as a joiner.

THE FELLING OF DIMMOCK'S CHIMNEY. HANLEY. June 15th '05

The Albion Works (the pottery of John Dimmock and Son) stood from the early 1800s until demolition in 1905. Occupying land between Stafford Street and Cheapside, the 'Felling of Dimmock's Chimney' must have been quite a spectacular sight, judging from this picture. The event drew a large crowd and postcards of it were produced and sold. At the Albion Square end of the site, the Olympia skating rink was built, later to become the Essoldo cinema. The cinema was demolished to make way for a C&A store. These pictures were taken from Albion Square at the top of Stafford Street, looking towards the top of Piccadilly.

THE FELLING OF DIMMOCK'S CHIMNEY. HANLEY June 15th 05.

Etruscan Series.

'Artes Etruriae Renascuntur' ('The Art of Etruria is Reborn') was the self-made motto with which Josiah Wedgwood christened his new Etruria works when it opened in 1769. Josiah purchased land previously known as the Ridge House Estate, which was at the time beautifully wooded land on the outskirts of Hanley. On this land he built his new pottery and a village to accommodate his workers. Inspired by Etruscan relics introduced to the country by Sir William Hamilton, he called the area Etruria. The house that Josiah built to live in is still standing and in use today as a hotel, but his factory was finally demolished in 1966, the pottery having moved to Barlaston in the previous years. Close proximity of the canal meant that wares from the factory could be transported safely to Liverpool, and then on by ship throughout the world.

This picture shows an example of a pottery technique that would have been used at Wedgwood's Etruria pottery. A young woman, or an older child, would turn the large wheel and a cotton belt would turn the potter's wheel or lathe. The person turning the wheel would be told to turn faster or slower to suit what the potter was doing, only resting when the potter removed the finished item.

A potter sitting at his wheel throwing a vase similar in shape to the famous Portland Vase. The potter would be paid for the number of items he had made each day, and in the early days of the industry he would pay a child to cut and weigh the clay ready for him to make the next pot. The same child would take the finished pot to the drying oven. *When I was a Child* by Charles Shaw is a factual account of his childhood in the Potteries in the early 1800s. It recounts that there were good and bad potters, as well as good and bad pottery owners. Josiah Wedgwood was considered a fair and good owner.

Above left: Loading a bottle oven at Wedgwood's pottery in Etruria. Placing saggers in a bottle oven is a difficult skill; each one is placed with great care so as to allow the heat from the fires to pass through each pillar of saggars, and so as to not fall over or damage the one under it. The correct placing of the saggars was so important that if they fell over the oven firing would have been ruined.

Above right: Firing one of the bottle ovens at Wedgwood's Pottery, Etruria. There were over fifteen bottle ovens at the factory. Josiah Wedgwood also built houses for his workers close to the pottery and his own house was built on the hillside overlooking all Etruria.

Pottery workers photographed in around 1920 taking a rest at Wedgwood's Pottery in Etruria.

Right: The Wedgwood family had been potters in Burslem for many generations, and it is appropriate that the 'Father of Potters' was born there, the 'mother town' of the Potteries. Josiah was born in July 1730, the youngest of thirteen children. Little is known about his childhood, only that his father died when Josiah was about nine years old. At about fourteen, Josiah was apprenticed to his oldest brother, Thomas Wedgwood. By 1759 Josiah was in his own pottery, and he opened his Etruria factory on 13 June 1769. Illness in his early life (he lost a leg due to polio) meant that he could not carry out all the tasks needed to produce pottery. This was to the benefit of the pottery industry, as it meant that he became more interested in the scientific aspects of producing pottery. He created a cream-coloured body, later known as Queen's Ware. He introduced the steam engine as a means of power to drive his clay, flint and stone mills. Much of the early production in Etruria was of Black Basalt Ware. Along with the Duke of Bridgwater, Wedgwood strove to improve the roads to and from North Staffordshire and was the driving force behind the scheme to ensure that the Trent and Mersey Canal passed through the Potteries.

Left: The Portland Vase (or Barberini Vase) was a crowning achievement for Josiah. The original is thought to have been made of cameo-glass around 25 BC. It took Josiah four years to perfect his masterpiece and in 1789 he proudly let Erasmus Darwin see the first one to be made in jasper.

Cauldon pottery is on the boundary between Hanley and Stoke. Situated on the side of the Caldon Canal between Stoke Road and what is now College Road. The factory was first built by Job Ridgway in about 1802.

This picture of Cauldon pottery was taken from the Stoke Road entrance as the workers went for lunch. Built by Job Ridgway, the pottery was later occupied by Bates & Co., and then by Bates & Westhead. In the first part of the twentieth century, Brown & Westhead produced pottery on the site. The old pottery factory has been demolished and the site is now occupied by Stoke-on-Trent College.

Bird's Eye View of the Potteries.

Looking towards Hanley, with Etruria gas works in the centre and Shelton New Road (renamed Newcastle Road in 1912) cutting across the middle of the picture. The bottle ovens of Twyfords Ltd and Cliffe Vale potteries can be seen on the right.

General View of the Potteries from Hanley.

From the side of the canal at Joiners Square, looking towards Wellington and Hanley. Very few of the large number of bottle ovens seen in the picture survive today. The Caldon canal runs across the middle of the picture.

WENGERS, LTD., ETRURIA, STOKE-ON-TRENT.

Telegrams: "Wengers Stoke-on-Trent."   Telephones No. **5126** and **5127** Stoke-on-Trent.

MANUFACTURERS OF
COLOURS, CHEMICALS, GLAZES, VITREOUS ENAMELS, MINERALS & MATERIALS
for the Pottery, Tile, Brick, Glass and Metal-Enamelling Industries.

AERIAL VIEW OF OUR WORKS AT ETRURIA

CARTE POSTALE.

WENGERS · LTD.

Fabricants de Couleurs et Produits Chimiques pour les Industries de la Céramique, du Verre et des Métaux Émaillés.

ETRURIA, STOKE-ON-TRENT

ANGLETERRE.

Above and right: Wengers Ltd were general providers of all colours and materials required in the pottery industry. These two post cards were sent to respective buyers and suppliers to confirm an order or to give a delivery date.

Opposite
Above: Etruria, with the gas-work's gas tank visible on the right, early 1920s. The ceramic materials factory of Wengers Ltd dominates the buildings in the picture.

Below: Wengers Ltd, founded in 1870 by Albert Francis Wenger. Originally based in Cobridge, he moved to this factory with more up-to-date equipment in 1900.

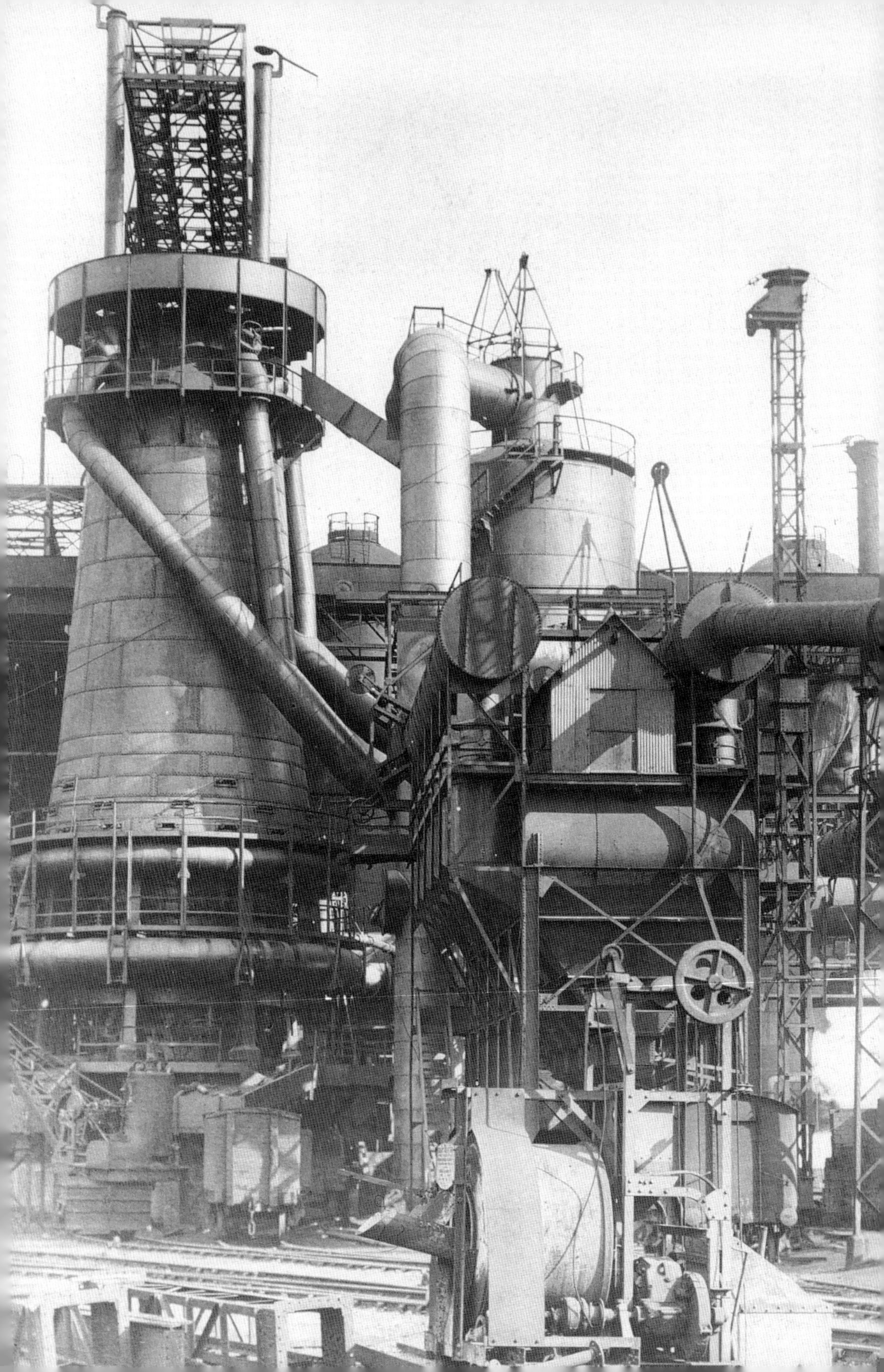

Born at the start of the Industrial Revolution, Granville Levison Gower (later Marquis of Stafford) brought the development of iron and steel to the Potteries in the early part of the nineteenth century. He built his first iron works next to Wedgwood's factory in Etruria and his son George took over the running of Shelton iron works in 1846 when he died. He was to remain in absolute control of the blast furnaces until his death in 1891. In 1899, vast improvements were made to the production of iron and steel. The result was the formation of new company Shelton Iron Steel and Coal Co. Ltd.

Above: a close-up of the base of the blast furnace.

Left: One of the blast furnaces at Shelton with the pig beds in the foreground left, *c*. 1890. In 1892 there were two steel furnaces at Shelton producing thirteen tons of steel eleven times a week. By 1905 the original two had been increased to eight, with a new smelting shop built beside the old ones.

Opposite: one of eight new blast furnaces built on the site by 1908.

One of the coking sheds at Shelton iron and coal works, where the coal was washed and prepared for coking in one of forty ovens, c. 1906. The coal was originally brought to the coking sheds by rail from one of the collieries in the Shelton area but later coal was railed in from local collieries such as Florence, Silverdale and Talke. Later at Etruria there were fifty-nine puddling furnaces and three 50cwt shingling hammers.

A blast furnace being tapped.

One of the many rolling mills at Shelton, which included a 22in. blooming mill, a 22in. bar mill and a 22in. plate mill. During 1914 a new 18in. rolling mill was built.

This photograph comes from a collection of pictures of Shelton's iron, steel and coal works. The chalk writing states that this picture is of the men from the 'Fitting Shop, Etruria, June 3rd 191?'. These men could either be workers at Shelton steel works or from the nearby colliery.

Shelton Colliery was right next to Shelton's iron, steel and coal works and the coal from here (and from many other coal mines in the area) fed the furnaces at the works. Later, coke was used in great quantities to fire the blast furnaces.

Opposite above: The Bath Street (now Garth Street) works entrance of Harrison & Son (Hanley) Ltd, *c.* 1920. Known as the Phoenix chemical works, Harrison's produced colours and glazes for the pottery industry, not only locally but world wide. The company won awards at Melbourne, Australia in 1880 and at the Worlds Fair in Chicago, USA in 1893 for its products.

Opposite below: Thomas W. Harrison worked for John Gerrard, who founded a colour works on this site in 1820. Part of the site was occupied by Old Hall pottery, but as the pottery glaze and colour business grew, so too did Gerrard's occupation of the surrounding buildings. When Gerrard died in about 1852, his wife sold the business to Harrison.

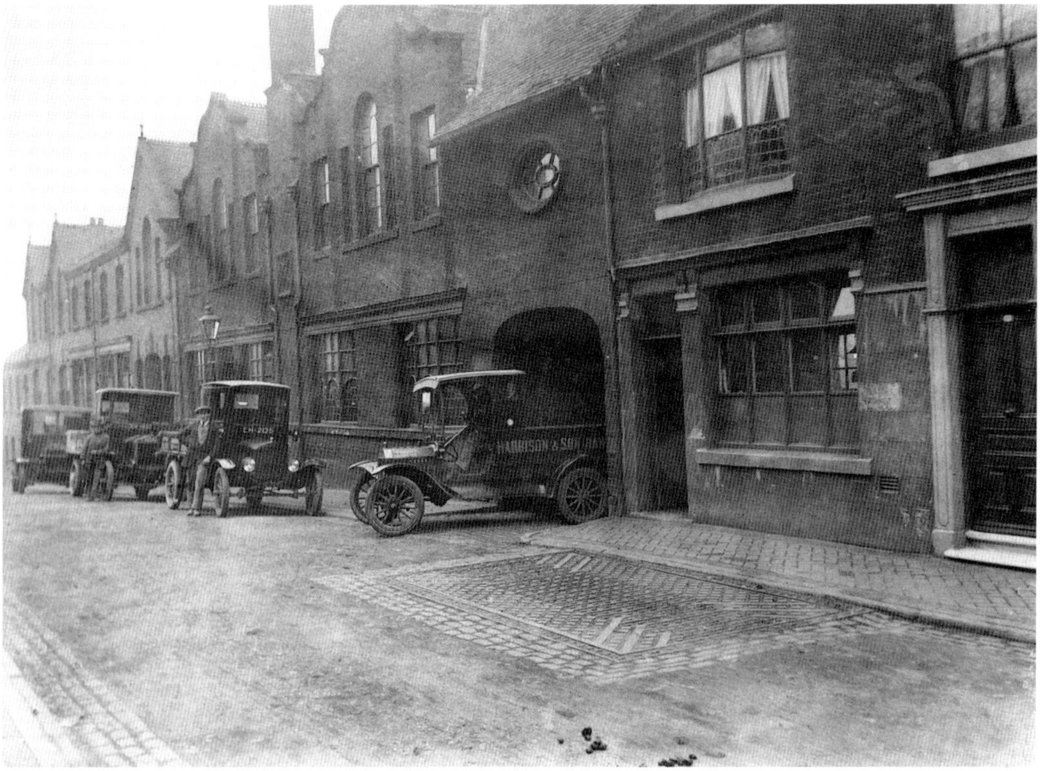

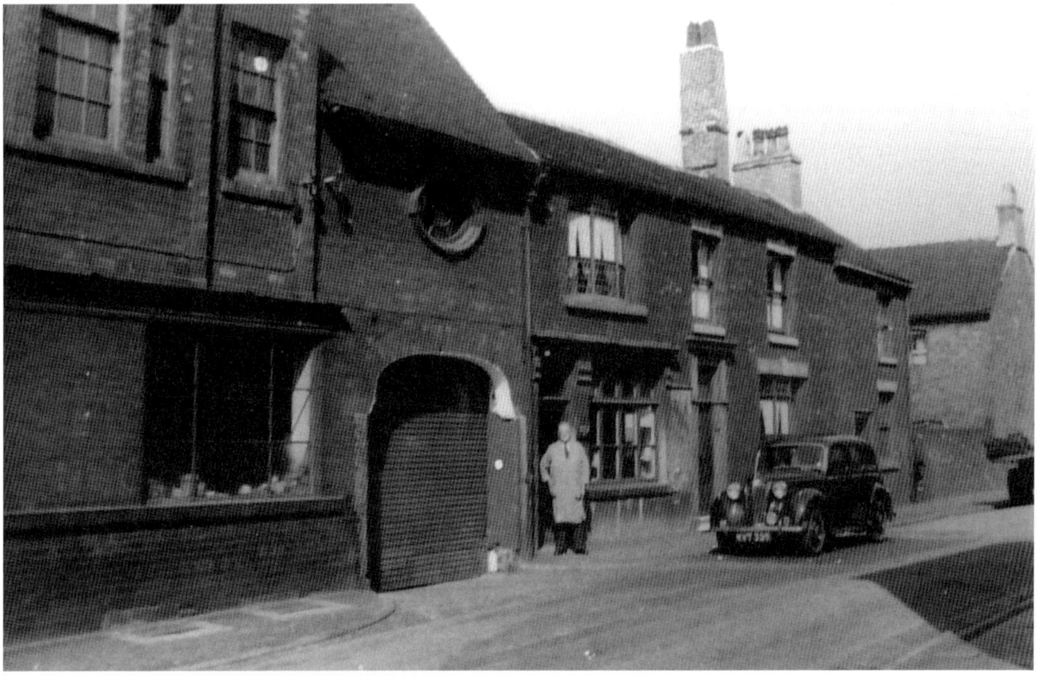

Number One Mill inside the factory of Harrison & Son (Hanley) Ltd, *c.* 1950. These ball mills are turned by flat belts driven from a main drive shaft. The drive shaft was driven by a steam engine that is now at the Gladstone Pottery Museum. The man on the far left is Reg Kilfoil, with his nephew Fred Kilfoil beside him. Both were maintenance fitters and each worked for the company for fifty years. Below is the more 'modern' Number Four Mill, built in the 1930s and powered by an electric motor.

Harrison's bought a new fleet of delivery lorries in the early 1930s. A few of these lorries were still in use in 1959.

This three-wheeled tanker is loading slip material for delivery to a local pottery. This picture was taken at Harrison's Joiners Square works in about 1950 and this energy-saving method of filling tankers by the power of gravity is still used today.

Henry Pidduck was born in Shrewsbury in 1813 and became apprentice to the Whitchurch clockmaker Thomas Joyce in 1827. By 1833 he was considered a master clockmaker. In 1841, he moved to Hanley to open a watchmaker's establishment in Market Square. In 1935, Pidduck's made the Hale Trophy (Blue Riband Trophy), presented to the fastest liner crossing the Atlantic. They also supplied much of the civic silverware for Hanley. The Blue Riband Trophy was displayed in Pidduck's window for many years, and the clock above Pidduck's was a Hanley landmark until the building was demolished in the 1970s. A Pidduck's jewellers shop survived in the Market Place until the late 1990s.

four

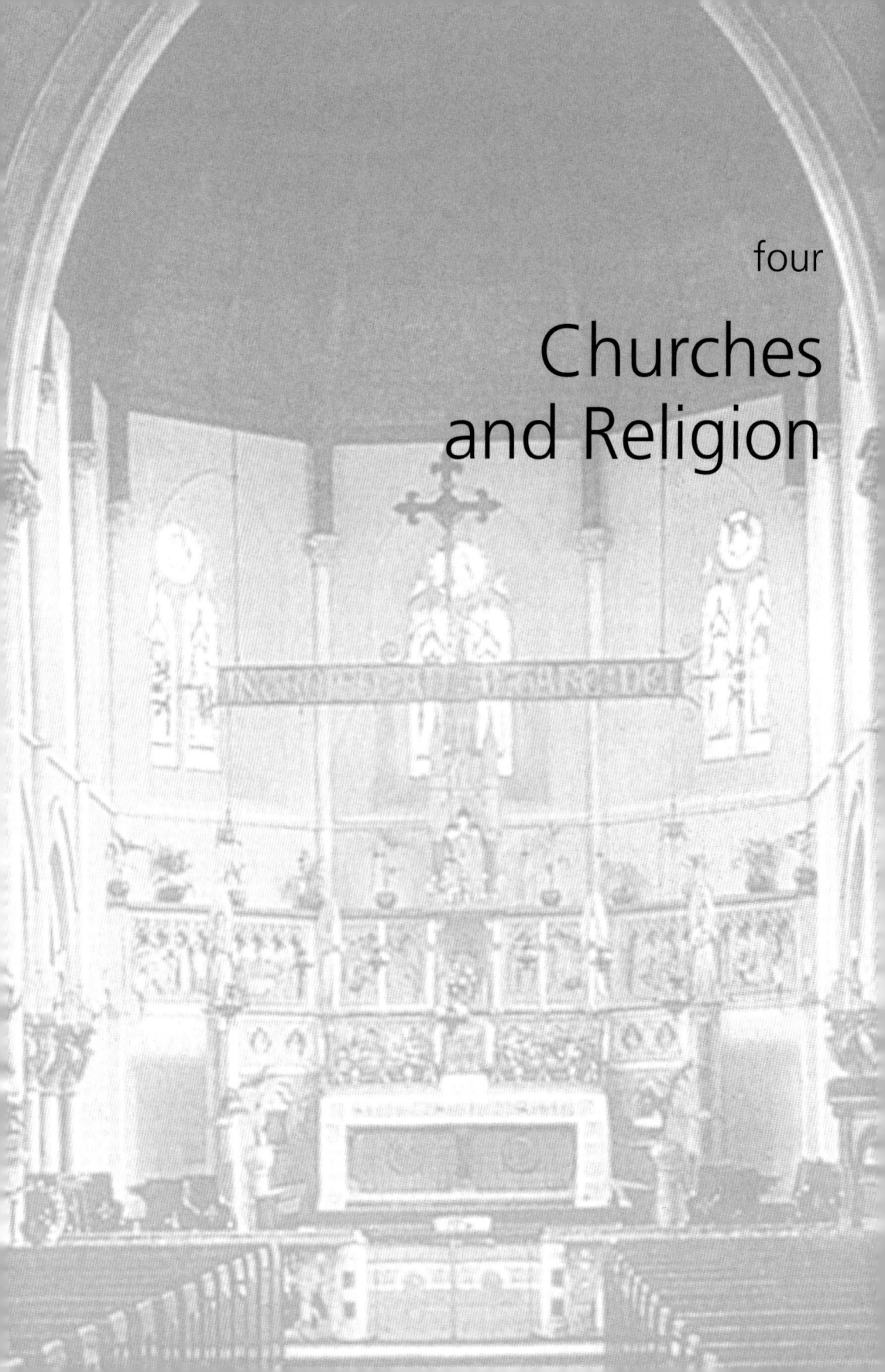

Churches
and Religion

In 1736 there were places of worship in Burslem, Norton, Bucknall and Stoke but none in Hanley. In 1737, John Bourne (from Newcastle) was on a visit to Hanley when, during a conversation with his host Mr Hollins at a dinner, the fact that Hanley did not have a church of its own came up. Bourne offered £500 towards the building of a place of worship in Hanley, providing that the rest of the sum required to build a church could be found by Hanley men. Mr Hollins added another £500 and Mr Adams of Birches Head Farm gave a piece of land upon which to build the church. By September of the next year, a church capable of seating 400 people had been built. The present church of St John, a large brick building with a tower 100 feet high was erected in 1788 on the site of the original church. The tower once contained a peal of eight bells.

The Independent Chapel in High Street, called the Tabernacle, was built in 1784, and was by 1800 regarded as the centre of Congregational work in North Staffordshire. The church was rebuilt in 1883 on the opposite side of the road to the original.

Shelton's church of St Mark is a large elegant stone building in the early English style. Erected in 1831 and consecrated by the Bishop of Lichfield in 1834, the tower is 120 feet high. Clay from the original foundation was used to make two jars and other small objects. One jar is in the possession of the church. Wellington St Luke's was built in 1851/52, and was consecrated on 6 July 1854.

Hanley had many Nonconformist Chapels and meeting houses, possibly the most famous being Bethesda Chapel in Albion Street, no longer used but the subject of a recent restoration television programme. In 1797, Bethesda Chapel was converted from a coach-house into a meeting house. However, it was too small to accommodate a growing congregation, and a new chapel was built in 1798 which seated 600 people. This attracted larger congregations and so the chapel was enlarged in 1811 by adding a semicircular extension at the rear. In 1818 the chapel was demolished to make way for the present Bethesda Chapel (built in 1819). By 1851 the chapel seated 2,500 worshipers and in 1859 the Corinthian pillars were added at the front. Sadly many of these places of worship have been demolished or are now used for other purposes.

St John Evangelist, on High Street (now Town Road) in Hanley, was first built in 1738, rebuilt in 1764 and then again in 1788. The church was recognised as a head of parish in 1890. The first curate-in-charge was the Revd John Middleton, an earnest Christian. He was a strong-willed man who, on one occasion, turned a mob from their intention to wreck Trentham Hall and persuaded them to return to their homes. A parsonage house was built in 1813, but was burnt down in August 1842 during the Chartist Riots; a new one was built in Old Hall Street. Nearly all the parish records were lost in the fire. This beautiful church lies empty today.

This Tabernacle church, was built in 1883, opposite an original Tabernacle church that was built in 1784. The original church was by 1800 regarded as the centre of Congregational work in North Staffordshire and was still standing in 1960, but was being used as a skating rink. The Tabernacle church pictured was a red brick and stone building which had a lecture hall, a school, a vestry and classrooms and was situated on High Street just above St John's church. The church closed in 1964 and was demolished some time later.

Bethesda chapel occupies the site of a preaching house erected in 1798, soon after the formation of the Methodist New Connection. The chapel is reported to have been built in 1819-20 from plans drawn up by a schoolmaster named Mr Perkins. In 1856, the pulpit and communion rail were renewed following designs by Robert Scrivener, and in 1859-60 a new frontage rendered in stucco was added. The building is made from red brick with yellow brick headers in 'Flemish Bond', whilst the roof is slate. The interior was refitted in the late nineteenth century.

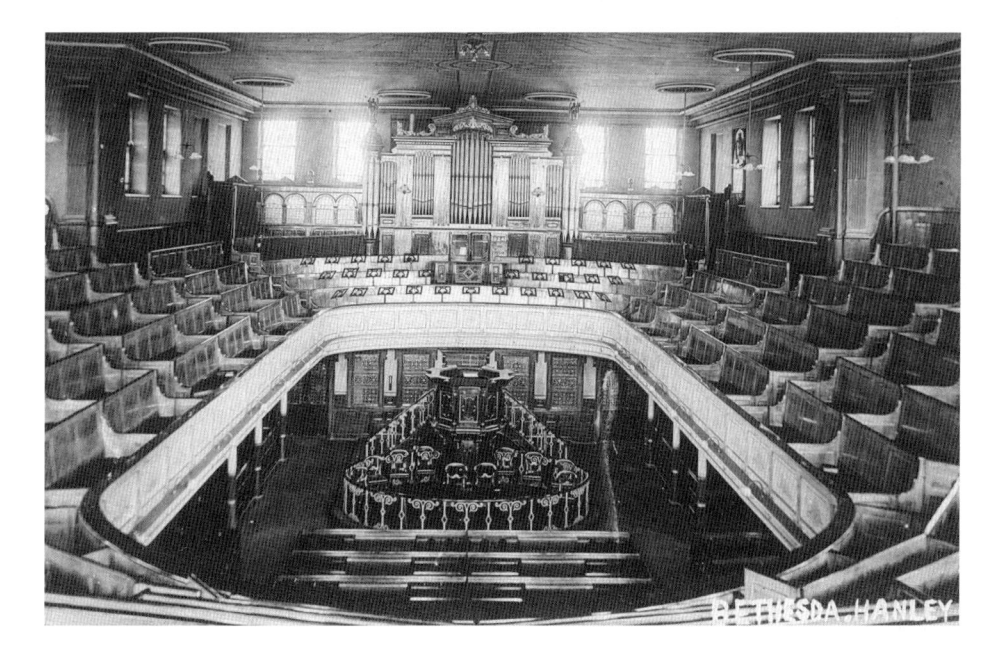

The foundation stone of St Mark's church in Shelton was laid on St Mark's Day in 1831, and was consecrated by the Bishop of Lichfield on 19 June 1834. The church was and probably still is the largest church in the diocese, seating some 2,100 worshipers. Built of freestone in the early English style, the 120ft tower originally had one bell and a clock. The main entrance is through a Gothic arch below the west side of the tower.

The chancel was rebuilt in 1866 as part of a major re-building programme organised by Revd Samuel Nevill. Included in the renovations were stalls for the clergy, benches with carved bookrests for the choir and all of the seating for the congregation. Electric lighting was introduced by Revd E. Duncan Boothman in 1895. The church is still used for worship today.

Known as the Church of the Sacred Heart, Hanley Roman Catholic church was built between 1889 and 1891 and was consecrated in 1911. Situated in Jasper Street, the original architect was H.V. Krolow, but the work was later taken over by R. Scrivener & Sons of Hanley.

The interior of the Church of the Sacred Heart has changed since this picture was taken during the mid-1950s. Extensive restoration work was carried out to the interior during the 1990s when it was returned to its original splendour with gold leaf and bright colours.

Left: On the corner of Marsh Street and Brunswick Street, this Primitive Methodist church was built in 1857, although it closed some time between 1884 and 1892. The main structure of the building still stands today, and was occupied by Blacks Outdoor Clothing and the Boy Scouts Association for a considerable period of time. Recently the building has been converted into a restaurant.

The first Primitive Methodist church in Hanley was built in 1824 on a site later occupied by Hanley railway station. Another church (today the site of the Theatre Royal) was sold to become a 'Peoples Hall', and in 1876 Hanley mayoress Mrs Baker laid a foundation stone for another Primitive Methodist church in Mount Street, Northwood. The Potteries played a major part in the upsurge of the Primitive Methodist Church.

Below: Providence Methodist church, on Providence Square. Originally built in 1839 on land given for a church by the Duchy of Lancaster, and modernised in 1924, the church was demolished in the 1960s.

Northwood Church.

Left: Designed by J. Trubshaw and built in 1848/49, Holy Trinity church in Northwood stands in an oasis of green, surrounded by housing. In 1849, Herbert Minton presented forty-six Staffordshire churches with tiles for the floor. Holy Trinity was one of them, although carpets cover the tiles today. The church was severely damaged by fire in 1949 but was restored and reopened for worship in 1950. The church is still in use today.

Below: Holy Trinity church, Northwood. These Service cards, which celebrated special events in the Christian calendar, were given out at many churches in the Potteries. Adults as well as children used to collect these beautiful cards and save them in cherished albums.

Holy Trinity, Northwood

Easter Services

EASTER DAY

Holy Communion at 7.0 a.m. and 8.0 a.m.

Sung Eucharist at 11.0 a.m.

Children's Service at 2.30 p.m.

Evensong and Sermon at 6.30 p.m.

Monday, Holy Communion at 9.0 a.m.

May you share in the joy of His Glorious Resurrection

Easter, 1946   R. N. TIMMS
Vicar

St Matthew's Church, Birches Rd.

Known affectionately to the people of Birches Head as 'the tin church', the original St Matthew's church was built of metal sheets and wood panels. Local people still remember the stove pot heating and wooden chairs instead of pews in the old church before it was replaced in the 1960s by a fine modern brick-built church. The 62nd City Scouts were based at St Matthew's church hall in nearby Addison Street.

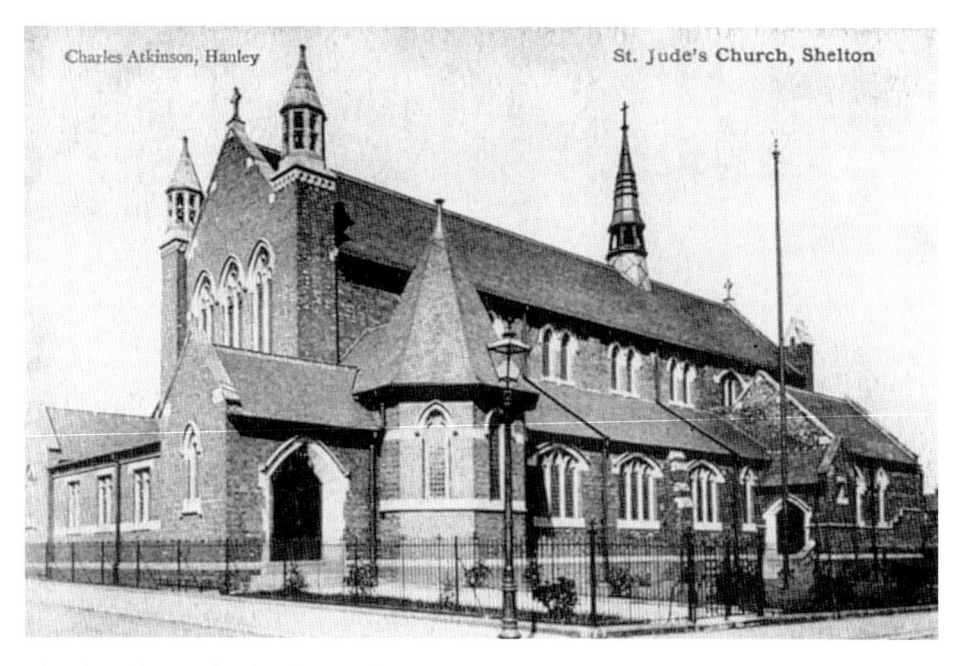

Charles Atkinson, Hanley — St. Jude's Church, Shelton

The chancel stone for the church of St Jude's in Shelton was ceremonially laid as early as 1879 and the church was repeatedly enlarged until 1896. The church was demolished in the late 1990s.

All Saints church on Joiners Square was built in about 1912 and is unique for having an extra outside pulpit. The original plans were for a larger church but lack of funds restricted the building to the size seen today. As a small Congregational church it was linked with St Luke's, but it later became a parish church in its own right.

Hanley cemetery chapel was erected in 1860 and consists of two chapels, one for Church of England followers and one for Nonconformists, with an archway in-between. Henry Ward & Son designed the building.

The Salvation Army Hanley Citadel Songster Brigade pictured outside the Citadel, c. 1945. The Salvation Army came to Hanley on 11 November 1881, when Major William Fawcett was appointed to commence work in the area. Meetings were held in Batty's Circus, which was on the present site of the main post office in Tontine Street. On 31 December 1881, Captain Rodney 'Gipsy' Smith took command and a February 1882 *War Cry* reported that 'things were happening in the town with people walking seven or eight miles to get converted'. There was a mission hall in Glass Street in 1898 and a Hanley Citadel in 1907, which is still in use today.

five

Parks

The Potteries area had to wait until 1888 for a public park, Longton Park being the first. After a public meeting held at the Victoria Hall in Hanley during 1890, the plan for Hanley Park was finally approved. These were the only parks for the residents of the Hanley area for some time, until Etruria Park came along in 1904 and Northwood Park was opened to the public in 1907.

Hanley Corporation purchased land known locally as Stoke Fields from the Shelton Old Hall Estate, on which to build Hanley Park. An unknown young architect named Thomas Mawson designed the park. This was his first public commission, and he worked very hard to obtain permission for his plans to be passed. The first sod in the twelve-acre Couldon Grounds (known locally as the flower park) was cut on 16 May 1892 and Alderman Hammers, mayor of Hanley, opened this part of Hanley Park on 26 July 1894. Henry Pidduck & Sons of Hanley made a silver key for the opening of the park. Alderman Tunnicliffe, then mayor of Hanley, opened the larger part of Hanley Park in 1897. Hanley Park hosted many community events, the first being the Hanley Park Fete, held in July 1897. This tradition still continues today, with Hanley Park being the home of many events held by the city during early June and July each year.

Thousands of people turned out on 29 September 1904 to witness the opening of the new eleven-acre Etruria Park. The most prominent feature of the park is the water fountain, donated by Alderman Jesse Shirley. The grey square stone fountain, with its pagoda-like top, originally had Wedgwood panels donated by the nearby Wedgwood pottery on opposite sides of the fountain. The Lady Mayoress was the first to drink from the fountain, wishing success to the park.

A new park for Northwood was envisaged and two possible locations were argued over bitterly. One group of people wanted the new park to be built on a twenty-acre part of Udalls Fields, situated on the border of Birches Head, Northwood and Abbey Hulton. Others thought that the new park should be built on Hall Fields, in the middle of Northwood. Though only ten acres were available, the Hall Fields site won the day and Northwood Park was opened in 1907 by Alderman T. Hampton, the mayor of Hanley.

The first part of Hanley Park to be opened was later known as the flower park, and contained many flowerbeds and a large conservatory. This long, wide promenade was a popular place to stroll along looking at the many wonderful flowers. When you consider that the Hanley area had many pottery bottle ovens belching out smoke, a walk in the park would have been a real treat.

The photographer placed these two children in front of one of the flowerbeds and arranged the picture to show the conservatory and the park's water fountain in the background. Though the conservatory is no longer there today, the water fountain remains and has now been incorporated into a very distinctive flowerbed.

The Stoke Road entrance to Hanley Park, which is between Stoke Road and what was called Victoria Road in 1900 (now College Road).

The large conservatory in the flower park held many exotic plants. Most people will remember the Banana Tree that had a prominent place in the conservatory. It was a popular place to visit in winter. The conservatory, along with its accompanying aviary, was pulled down some time in the 1980s.

Hanley Park's five-acre ornamental lake has been a haven for people and wildlife since it was built. Fishing and boating were favourite weekend pastimes for many hard-working potters. At one time the park lake was the home of many ornamental ducks and a favourite childhood treat was to go 'down the park and feed the ducks'.

Hanley Park.

When the park first introduced rowing boats on the lake they proved very popular and many courting couples have spent a Sunday afternoon on this lake. In the late 1950s and '60s there were two-seater paddleboats that children could use and an area of the lake was roped off for these boats.

The bandstand was built in 1896, paid for by Mr George Howson, a local pottery owner. The glass panels were removable, and they created a sunhouse when the bandstand was not in use. Bands were a great attraction, playing religious music on Sundays and popular music at other times. Many famous brass bands have played to an appreciative audience seated around this bandstand. The park pavilion can be seen in the background.

Hanley Park boasts a large oval bowling green where, at the turn of the nineteenth century, you could play bowls with your friends for about threepence an hour. In the 1960s you could have a game by hiring a set of bowls if you had none of your own to play with.

The park had many large flowerbeds. In the early days of the park, local flower-lovers were encouraged to grow flowers in a few square feet of space and many Victorian horticulturists attained a degree of excellence while helping in the park gardens. The pavilion was opened in 1896 and was designed by Mr Dan Gibson. It contains a central hall with tea rooms for ladies and for gentlemen at each end. Behind the central hall is a kitchen with living quarters for a park attendant above. The pavilion was used when events like the Hanley Flower Show were held in the park.

The park was the home of many events and public shows, including the Potteries Horse Parade. These two gentlemen are the proud winners of the 1923 RSPCA Cup and the Champions Cup, respectively. In 1930 the Wedgwood bicentenary was held at the park and events are still held in the park today.

NORTHWOOD PARK.

Opened in 1907 (the same year as the jubilee of the borough) Northwood Park is built on sloping ground in a terrace arrangement amid housing on land once called Hall Fields. Original designs for the park show, along with the usual bandstand and bowling green, a quoits lawn, a fernery and separate playgrounds for boys and girls. This picture was taken from Baskerville Road.

Etruria Park, Hanley.

Etruria Park is the smallest of Hanley's parks, built on land opposite Wedgwood's pottery, which can be seen in the background of this picture. Opened on 29 September 1904, the most prominent feature is this magnificent water fountain, donated by Mr Jesse Shirley.

six

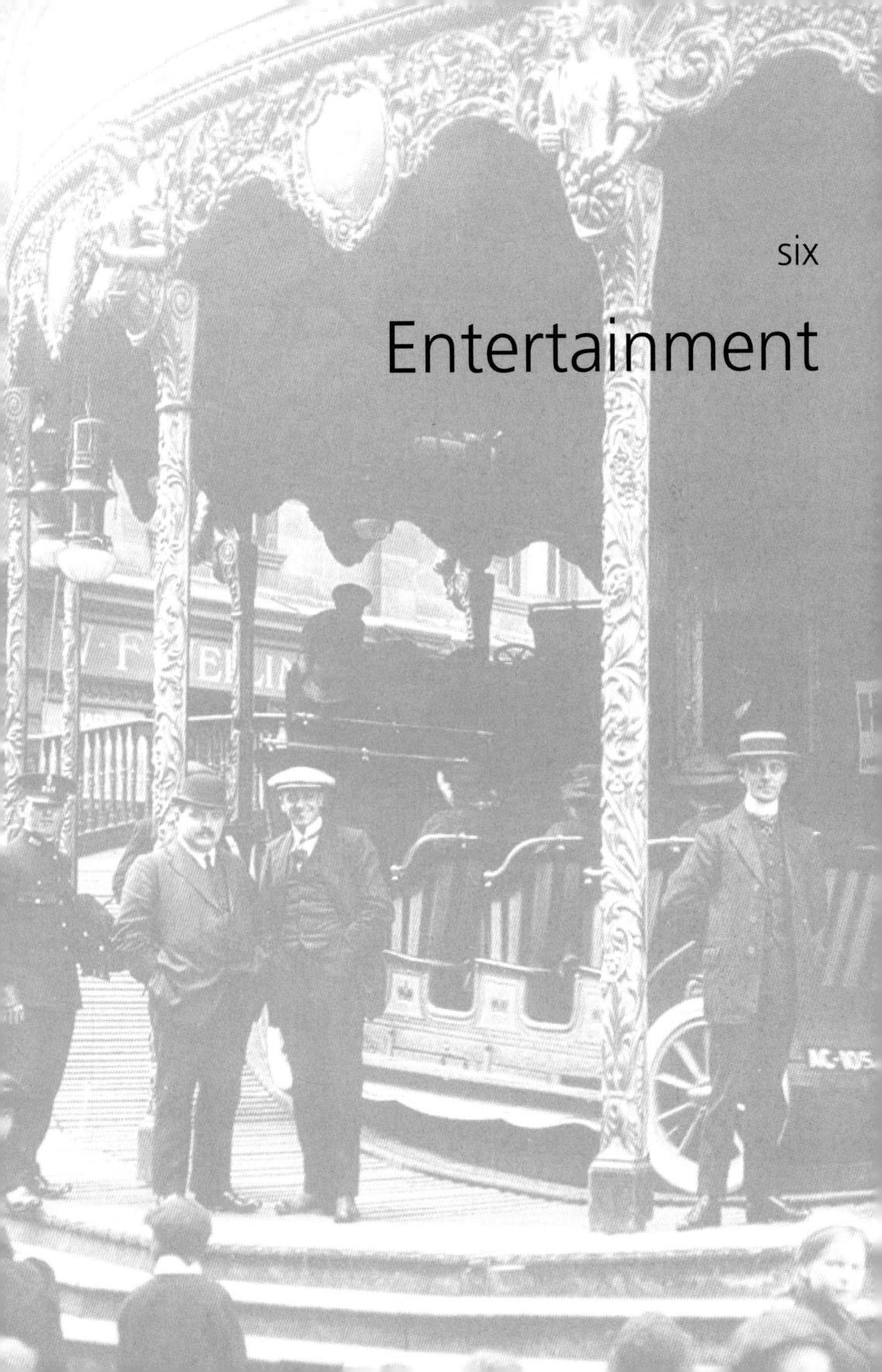

Entertainment

Not counting the large number of public houses and ale houses, Hanley was a rich area for the public to be entertained. In the early days, bear baiting was organised outside the Albion public house and the town's ducking pool was situated outside Ye Olde French Horn in the centre of Hanley. Music halls (some of which became theatres, silent film theatres, and cinemas) and the many public halls put on a rich array of entertainment. Hanley boasted its own skating rink up until the 1960s, and Port Vale Football Club played at the Recreation Ground behind St John's church up until 1952, both within close walking distance of Market Square. In 1823, Hanley even had its own racecourse, which occupied land where the Festival Business Park is today. The last race meeting was held in 1859.

Live entertainment was catered for in the many small music halls and theatres in Hanley, the largest of which were The Theatre Royal, The Grand Theatre and The Victoria Hall. Sadly The Victoria Hall is the only one of these old places of entertainment still operating as a theatre today, although The Theatre Royal has recently reopened as a public house and nightclub.

The Theatre Royal had a lively past. It was first opened in 1851 in a building that had been a Primitive Methodist chapel. Originally called the People's Hall, and later the Potteries Royal Theatre, the original building was demolished in 1870 when the first brick of a new theatre was laid, opening that same year and called The Theatre Royal. However, the building was not big enough, so architect Frank Matcham was commissioned to design a new theatre seating 2,600 people. This building was opened on 6 August 1887 but burned down in 1949. A new theatre was built and had a grand opening on 14 August 1951, with Annette MacDonald starring in *Annie Get Your Gun*.

Frank Matcham was the most famous theatre architect of the day and also designed The Grand Theatre of Varieties and Circus in Trinity Street. Built in 1897, the theatre had a revolving stage and could seat up to 2,500 people. Moving pictures were on the bill as early as 1899, but the theatre burned down in 1932, shortly after it was officially converted into a cinema. Five years later the present building was opened as the Odeon cinema. One of the first Hanley theatres to introduce 'Cinematograph' was the Empire Palace in New Street, in 1896.

Many famous local footballers started their career playing for one of Hanley's football teams. Port Vale was the local professional team but there were many minor league teams for the public to watch, including Hanley Swifts, Northwood Boys Social Club and Old Hanliensian FC.

The people of Hanley have observed a Wakes festival since the very beginning of the community. This ancient festival first began as a church procession on the first Sunday in August. During the nineteenth century, festivities such as fairground attractions would be set up in a number of Hanley's many squares. Trentham Day was also an important event in the Wakes Week calendar; Trentham Thursday, as it was also known, was a day when the Duke of Sutherland would open his grounds to the people of the Potteries and every type of vehicle, from donkey cart to landau, would descend on his Trentham estate. Wakes Week was still celebrated well into the twentieth century, when Pat Collins' fair would set up on ground off Regent Road, although later many people spent the Wakes Week holiday at the seaside.

Above: Known as the Royal Pottery Theatre, the Theatre Royal in Hanley began life in 1857 when a Primitive Methodist meeting hall in Brunswick Street was acquired to be used as a theatre. In about 1875, a new, larger theatre was built on the same spot with a new entrance in Pall Mall. These developments were funded by licensee Mr Windley. Small cottages were knocked down in Pall Mall so that the new building extended between there and Brunswick Street. The site of the old theatre became the location of the new stage and dressing rooms, with the auditorium and entrance using the rest of the land. This building was enlarged again in 1888 and again in 1894, but was destroyed by fire in June 1949; the present Theatre Royal building had a grand opening in August 1951. Hanley's Theatre Royal has closed and re-opened a number of times in the last quarter of the twentieth century, finally closing as a theatre in 2000.

Below: The Theatre Royal in Hanley became a favourite venue for Music Hall stars and many famous entertainers of the Edwardian era appeared there. Music Hall stars such as Marie Lloyd, Hetty King, George Elliot and Hanley's own Gertie Gitana all performed in the theatre. Many of the plays came straight from London, and postcards advertising each show were produced showing a picture of the star or a scene from the play, along with the time and date of the performance. The Theatre Royal was regarded as one of the top-ten theatres in Britain and the Potteries crowd as being the most appreciative audience. During the 1960s many pop stars appeared at the theatre, and during the 1980s and 1990s it was home to *The Rocky Horror Show*.

GRAND THEATRE, TRINITY STREET, HANLEY.

A rival to the Theatre Royal was the Grand Theatre of Varieties and Circus on the corner of Trinity Street and Foundry Street. Opened in August 1898 at a cost of £20,000, the building was designed by Frank Matcham and built by Thomas Goodwin of Hanley. The Grand was noted for having a stage 63ft wide and 44ft deep that could be removed. This was particularly beneficial when the circus came to town as the circus arena could replace the stage. The theatre always seemed to have had moving pictures on the bill, but shortly after it was converted into a cinema in 1932 the theatre was destroyed by fire. The final programme at the Grand Theatre was the film *The Mad Genius* starring John Barrymore. It was rebuilt as the Odeon cinema and opened in February 1937 with the film *Educated Evans*. The Odeon showed many classic films (such as *South Pacific* and *The Sound of Music*) for long runs, before finally closing in 1975. In 1952 it held the provincial premiere of the film of Arnold Bennett's book *The Card*, which contained many scenes filmed in the Potteries.

112

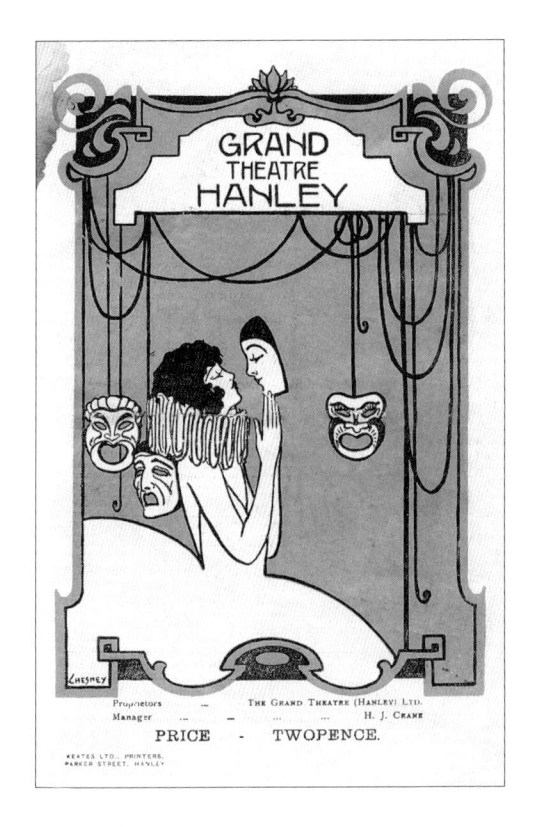

Above left: The Grand Theatre was much more a light entertainment theatre than its rival the Theatre Royal. A typical evening's entertainment would include magicians, jugglers and novelty acts along with popular singers of the day. Some weeks were devoted to circus acts, and most bills had a showing of new silent films and comedy plays from London.

Above right: Like many other theatres, the Grand sold postcards advertising forthcoming programmes. Many of these postcards were issued by the stars of the programme, and the theatre's name and the dates of the performances were stamped on later. Mr and Mrs G.H. Elliot were very popular performers during the early part of the twentieth century.

Right: Harry J. Crane was the manager of the Grand Theatre in Hanley during the 1920s, overseeing much of the early transition from live entertainment to moving pictures.

Roller skating was a very popular pastime in Hanley. One of the first skating rinks in Hanley was the Olympia, situated at the top of Stafford Street and managed in 1912 by Mr P. Collins (left). During the 1920s, Percy Swain was the popular manager of the rink. In 1934 the Ideal skating rink opened in Town Road, and when it closed in 1974 there were many articles in the *Sentinel* newspaper denouncing the decision. A petition with over 2,000 names was given to the council asking for help to open another skating rink in Hanley and there was even a protest march through the centre of the town. Another rink opened in the old Roxy cinema in 1981, but it closed again in 1984.

The Victoria Hall in Hanley has long been a source of rich entertainment for the people of the Potteries. Opened in 1888 to commemorate the Golden Jubilee of Queen Victoria, the Victoria Hall is situated behind the town hall with the main entrance in Bagnall Street. Noted for being one of the best acoustic concert halls in the country, the Victoria Hall has played host to famous singers such as Paul Robeson, Richard Tauber and Beniamino Gigli, as well as great musicians such as Rachmaninoff. Great orchestras also played there, including the Hallé Orchestra, conducted by Sir Thomas Beecham and later by John Barbirolli. The London Philharmonic Orchestra was a frequent visitor during the early 1940s, conducted by Dr Malcolm Sargent. Today the Victoria Hall is still an important concert venue, with many of today's stars performing there.

The Hospital Sunday Festival, held in Hanley Park, was an annual event that the people of the Potteries looked forward to. There were many fund-raising events and competitions held on Hospital Sunday throughout the area and a fair always came to Hanley during the week.

This merry-go-round was erected in Parliament Square for Hospital Sunday. The old Hanley meat market can be seen in the background. Even today, there is sometimes a travelling fairground attraction situated in Parliament Square for a weekend.

An ancient festival held on the first Sunday in August consisting of a procession through Hanley to a church, later became a week-long celebration known as Wakes Week. Stalls of all kinds were set up in Hanley during the week. Taken at the very beginning of the twentieth century, this picture shows Fountain Square with Market Square in the background.

Many of Hanley's large open squares were occupied by fairground attractions such as merry-go-rounds, bazaar stalls, shooting galleries and even peep shows. Tontine Square, *c.* 1898.

The first record of Port Vale Football Club was in an 1880 edition of the *Staffordshire Sentinel*, though it is believed that the club was founded in 1879 in the Longport area of Burslem. In 1886, Vale moved to Cobridge and moved again around 1912 to the Old Recreation Ground in Hanley. In the summer of 1950 Vale moved back to Burslem. This picture was taken in around 1936.

The 1947/48 Port Vale team finished eighth in Division Three (South), and it was the first professional season for Ronnie Allen (seated front row, far left), who scored thirteen goals. He was transferred to West Bromwich Albion in 1950 and later played for England.

There were many very good minor league football teams in the Hanley area, the best-known being Hanley Swifts, who had their ground in the Botany Bay area of Northwood. Hanley Swifts played in the North Staffordshire & District League from about 1897 and by 1911 had won the League 9 times. They played until the First World War, when many teams were suspended and never reformed.

Northwood Boys won the North Staffordshire Amateur Minor League Cup in 1936 and were joint Minor League champions in the same year.

seven

Hanley District

In the early eighteenth century Hanley was a small market town, but with the advance of the pottery industry it became one of the largest towns in North Staffordshire. As early as 1714 Hanley and Shelton were bracketed together but it was not until just over one hundred years later that an Act of Parliament formed them into a market town. By 1769 Mr Wedgwood's Etruria was also talked about as a town alongside Hanley as the community grew. Many of the Hanley pottery owners had large houses built in the countryside of Sneyd Green and Northwood, with others building their houses in Shelton and Etruria. In 1901 the County Borough of Hanley extended its parliamentary voting area to cover the wards of Etruria, Hope, Providence, Northwood, Wellington, Park and Cauldon, an area of 1,768 acres with a population of over 61,000 people. By the federation of Stoke-on-Trent in 1910, Hanley also included Sneyd Green, Birches Head, Joiners Square and a small portion of Cobridge within the Hanley borough boundary.

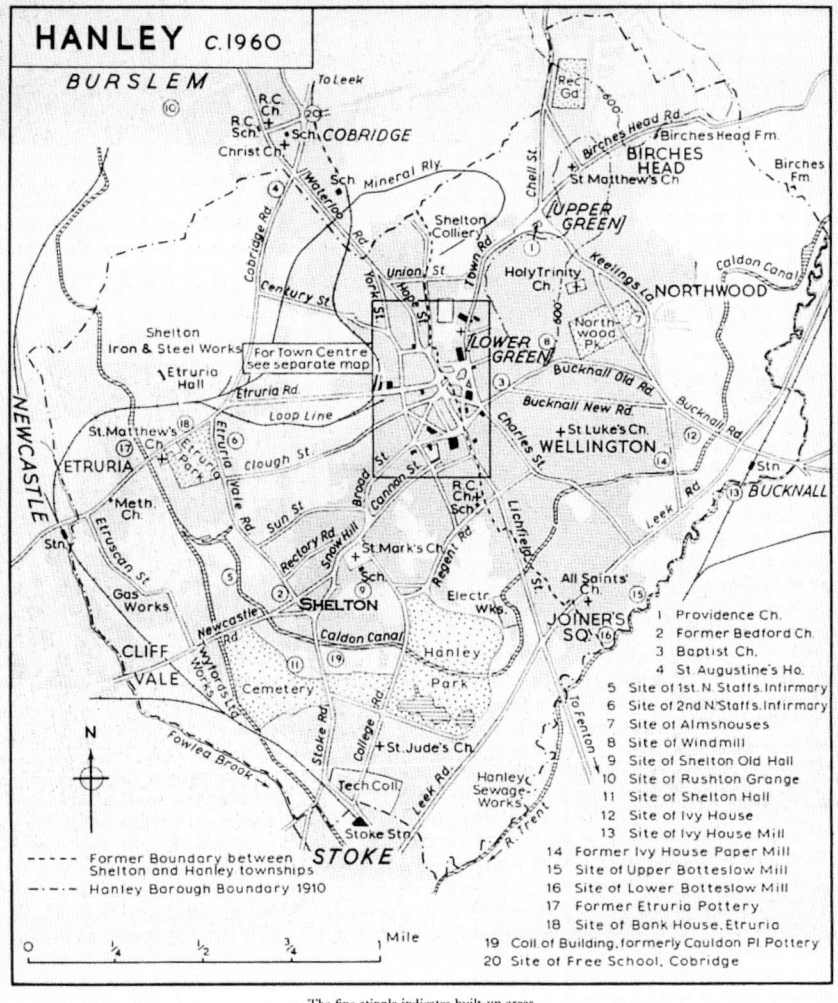

A map of Hanley, c. 1960. (Reproduced from the *Victoria County History, Staffordshire Volume VIII*, p. 172, by permission of the Executive Editor.)

Out of Hanley towards Shelton is Victoria Square, dominated on the Hanley side by the Victoria Hotel, seen here in the left-hand corner and partially hidden by the tram with three private houses to the right. The hotel was once the home of the North Staffordshire Museum. Victoria Square was also home to the headquarters of the Shropshire and Staffordshire Royal Garrison Artillery Volunteers 3rd and 4th Batteries, with a compliment of 421 men.

From Victoria Square the tram passes Shelton church, then the Bell and Bear public house at the top of Snow Hill before heading down towards Stoke. Little change has been made to the frontage of the Bell and Bear, and even Lewis & Sproston still have a flower shop next door.

SNOW HILL, SHELTON.

With the Bell and Bear in the background, the tram trundles along on its journey towards Stoke, accompanied here by a rider on a horse. The houses on the left still stand today, joined together as a hotel.

Snow Hill, Shelton, Hanley.

Snow Hill from the top of Howard Place, looking towards the Bell and Bear. The wall on the right surrounds Richmond House, for a long time the home of Mr A.R. Moody MBCM, a physician and surgeon, now Hanley Masonic Hall.

Shops have replaced the terraced houses on the right of this picture, while the tram passenger shelter on the left has been replaced with a roundabout. These are the only changes that have occurred in Howard Place since this picture was taken in about 1910. Shelton church overlooks the scene.

The large house in the top left of this 1920s picture of Howard Place is The Elms, which was once owned by Mr R.G. Howson, a manufacturer of sanitary wares. George Howson was born in 1818 and started his own business in 1865 at Eastwood. He died in 1896 and his sons took over the business. Today the house is a restaurant.

This picture was taken half-way down Lichfield Street looking towards Hanley and Joiners Square. Many of the houses in the picture still stand today and recent roadworks exposed cobbles and tramlines.

A view of Joiners Square taken from the canal looking towards the Wellington district of Hanley. The foreground of this picture used to be Harrison & Son's Joiners Square factory, where much of the clay used in the Potteries was mixed and blended to suit the industry. Today it is owned by Johnson Matthey, who continues the business of making quality ceramic materials for the pottery industry.

On the northern edge of Hanley is Sneyd Green and this prominent shop on the corner of Hanley Road and Buxton Street was owned by Henry Bull, grocer and postmaster of Sneyd Green in 1912. It is still a post office today.

Before Sneyd Green post office on Hanley Road is Chell Street and the Cheshire Cheese Inn. This large inn was rebuilt in 1898, but a Cheshire Cheese public house stood on the site as early as 1851, when the owner was Philip Poole. This picture was taken to celebrate Samuel Mayer taking over the ownership of the inn just after 1900. This popular inn has the same name today.

Next from Sneyd Green is Birches Head. This old lane leads from Hanley to Abbey Hulton. Except for the horse and cart, this picture could have been taken today. The corner shop that belonged to Barker & Stevenson in 1912 was later owned for a long time by the Mayor family.

Market Place.

With Greetings from HANLEY.

Park Lake.

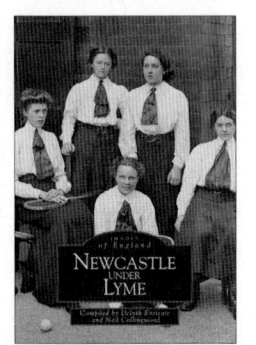

Other local titles published by Tempus

Newcastle-under-Lyme
DELYTH ENTICOTT AND NEIL COLLINGWOOD

Located at the confluence of several major road transport routes, Newcastle developed as a town following the strategic siting of a castle there in the twelfth century. A large produce market was established outside the castle and, because of this, Newcastle became for centuries the most important town in the area. This fascinating collection of over 200 photographs explores the historic Borough of Newcastle-under-Lyme, covering not only the urban history of the borough but also the everyday aspects of life in its rural districts.
0 7524 2074 7

Stoke City Football Club
TONY MATTHEWS

As founder members of the Football League, Stoke City FC has a long and proud tradition. This book illustrates its impressive history with over 200 images, including old team groups, action shots, player portraits and programme covers, each supported by a detailed caption from the football statistician and experienced sports writer, Tony Matthews. Included in the selection are pictures featuring various promotion seasons, cup runs and other significant events sure to appeal to older fans and younger supporters interested in this club's fine sporting heritage.
0 7524 1698 7

Burslem
THE BURSLEM HISTORY CLUB

Using over 200 evocative images, this book documents the people and places of Burslem, the Mother Town of the Potteries. Many of Burslem's grand Victorian buildings are included, as well as factories, schools and churches. Significant events are also recorded, such as the Sneyd Pit disaster of 1942. This pictorial history offers a reminder of another age and provides a valuable insight into how people lived and worked in this industrial community.
0 7524 3456 X

Biddulph: Volume II
DEREK WHEELHOUSE

This absorbing collection of over 200 archive images, tracing some of the changes and developments in Biddulph over the last century. This volume highlights some of the social events that have taken place during this time, including occasions such as the Biddulph Moor Carnival, as well as aspects of everyday life, from schools and shops to transport and leisure pursuits. This book is a valuable pictorial history which will awaken nostalgic memories for some, while offering a unique glimpse of the past for others.
0 7524 3463 2

If you are interested in purchasing other books published by Tempus, or in case you have difficulty finding any Tempus books in your local bookshop, you can also place orders directly through our website
www.tempus-publishing.com